Contents

ISLAMOPHOBIA AND ANTI-SEMITISM

ISLAMOPHOBIA
—— *and* ——
ANTI-SEMITISM

Hillel Schenker
Ziad Abu-Zayyad
editors

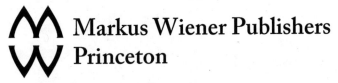

Markus Wiener Publishers
Princeton

Published in coöperation with the Palestine–Israel Journal.

Chapters 1–6, 9, 11, 12, 18, and 19 are reprinted from the *Palestine-Israel Journal of Politics, Economics and Culture* 12, nos. 2 & 3 (2005).

Chapter 8, "Bridging the Unbridgeable" by Dan Bar-On and Saliba Sharsar, is reprinted from the *Palestine-Israel Journal* 11, no. 1 (2004). Chapter 10, "Fear of the Other" by Hanna Biran, is reprinted from the *Palestine-Israel Journal* no. 4 (Autumn 1994). Chapter 15, "The Arab Image in Hebrew School Textbooks" by Daniel Bar-Tal, and chapter 17, "Schoolbooks in the Making" by Sami Adwan, are reprinted from the *Palestine-Israel Journal* 8, no. 2 (2001). Chapter 16, "The Politicization of Palestinian Children: An Analysis of Nursery Rhymes" by Nafez and Laila Nazzal, is reprinted from the *Palestine-Israel Journal* 3, no. 1 (1996).

Chapter 13, "Learning all the wrong facts" by Akiva Eldar, was originally published in *Haaretz*, December 9, 2004, and is reprinted by permission of the author.

Chapter 14, "Incitement in Israeli and Palestinian Textbooks" by Nadia Nasser-Najjab, was originally published in *Palestine Report*, March 9, 2005, and is reprinted by permission of the author.

For information write to:
Markus Wiener Publishers, 231 Nassau Street, Princeton, NJ 08542
www.markuswiener.com

Cover and book design by Wangden Kelsang

Library of Congress Cataloging-in-Publication Data

Islamophobia and anti-Semitism / edited by Hillel Schenker and Ziad
    Abu-Zayyad.
    p. cm.
    Includes bibliographical references.
    ISBN-13: 978-1-55876-402-6 (hardcover : alk. paper)
    ISBN-10: 1-55876-402-X (hardcover)
    1. Antisemitism--History--21st century. 2. Islamophobia--History--21st century. 3. Arab-
Israeli conflict--Influence. I. Schenker, Hillel. II. Abu Zayyad, Ziad.
    DS145.I85 2006
    305.6'97095694--dc22

                                                                    2006015715
ISBN-13: 978-1-55876-403-3 (paperback)
ISBN-10: 1-55876-403-8 (paperback)

Printed in the United States of America on acid-free paper.

INTRODUCTION

Anti-Semitism and Islamophobia are two sicknesses that plague our modern world. Both are based upon simplistic stereotypes, and they fan the flames of fear and hatred against the "other." Thus Jews and Muslims serve frequently as convenient scapegoats for many of society's ills and leaders' misguided agendas.

If the international community was under the illusion that the end of World War II and the establishment of the United Nations would bring an end to these plagues, it was sadly mistaken. Both are very much with us in the twenty-first century.

The post-9/11 world, the Iraq War, the breakdown of homogeneous societies in Europe, the rise of fundamentalisms, and the lack of a resolution to the Israeli-Palestinian conflict have only served to exacerbate these two phenomena. Among the controversial terms in vogue today are "The New Anti-Semitism" and "The Clash of Civilizations."

We advocate the dialogue rather than the clash of civilizations.

The *Palestine-Israel Journal*, a unique joint venture run by a group of prominent Israeli and Palestinian academics and journalists, felt it was necessary to devote an entire issue to this problem. This was not coincidental. Anti-Semitism and Islamophobia are breeding hatred and creating more difficulties in the face of any serious effort to solve the Israeli-Palestinian conflict. They are threatening to transform it from a political to a religious conflict. They target both Muslims and Jews simply because of their religious affiliation. This casts its shadow on the Middle East and clouds the judgment of anyone attempting to resolve the conflict. This is true in the region and in the broad international arena. Anti-Semitism and Islamophobia create many innocent victims in both communities and undermine the potential constituencies for peace and a political resolution of the conflict.

The editors of the *Palestine-Israel Journal* (www.pij.org), an independent quarterly based in Jerusalem, act in accordance with the following mission statement: "The *Palestine-Israel Journal* aims to shed light on, and analyze freely and critically, the complex issues dividing Israelis and Palestinians. It also devotes space to regional and international affairs. The *Journal's* purpose is to promote rapprochement and better understanding between peoples, and it strives to discuss all issues without prejudice and taboo."

This volume is based on articles which appeared in our special issue devoted to Anti-Semitism and Islamophobia (vol. 12, nos. 2 & 3, 2005), along with relevant articles from past issues, and a few new articles. We hope that it will make a meaningful contribution to clarifying the origins, meaning, and implications of these two scourges, and believe it will serve as a constructive resource and tool for students, academics, activists, community leaders, and opinion- and decision-makers.

Hillel Schenker *and* Ziad Abu Zayyad

CHAPTER ONE

ISLAMOPHOBIA
A New Word for an Old Fear

Imam Dr. Abduljalil Sajid

"And they ill-treated them [believers] for no other reason except that they believed in Allah" (Al-Qur'an 85–8).

The term "Islamophobia" was first used in print in 1991 and was defined in the Runnymede Trust Report (the Runnymede Trust Commission on British Muslims and Islamophobia, 1997) as "unfounded hostility towards Islam, and therefore fear or dislike of all or most Muslims." The word has been coined because there is a new reality which needs naming—anti-Muslim prejudice has grown so considerably and so rapidly in recent years that a new item in the vocabulary is needed so that it can be identified and acted against.

The term "Islamophobia" is, admittedly, not ideal. It was coined by way of analogy to "xenophobia" and can be characterized by the belief that all or most Muslims are religious fanatics, have violent tendencies towards non-Muslims, and reject such concepts as equality, tolerance, and democracy. It is a new form of racism whereby Muslims, an ethno-

1

religious group, not a race, are, nevertheless, constructed as a race. A set of negative assumptions is made of the entire group to the detriment of members of that group. During the 1990s many sociologists and cultural analysts observed a shift in racist ideas from ones based on skin color to ones based on notions of cultural superiority and otherness.

Manifestations

In Britain as in other European or Western countries, manifestations of anti-Muslim hostility can be seen to include such features as verbal and physical attacks on Muslims in public places,[1] and attacks on mosques and desecration of Muslim cemeteries. It can be seen in widespread and routine negative stereotyping in the media and everyday discourse in ways that would not be acceptable if the reference were, for example, to Jewish or black people; or in negative stereotypes and remarks in speeches by political leaders, implying that Muslims are less committed than others to democracy and the rule of law—the claim in Britain, for example, that Muslims must choose between "the British way" and "the terrorist way."[2] It can also manifest itself in discrimination in recruitment and employment practices and in the workplace; in delay and inertia in responding to Muslim requests for cultural sensitivity in education, in healthcare, and in protection against incitement to hatred; and in curtailment of civil liberties that disproportionately affect Muslims.

Violent language

September 11, 2001, and the days that followed produced strong feelings amongst non-Muslims as well as among Muslims. When people feel powerless and frustrated they are prone to hit out with violent language: "You don't belong here," or "Get out of my country now; England is for white civilized English people!" are examples of the kind of violent language that was used in e-mail messages to the Muslim Council of Britain immediately following the attacks. These messages are significant, for they expressed attitudes and perceptions that are widespread amongst non-Muslims and that are recurring components of Islamophobia.

An alleged factor, some argue, that fuels Islamophobia is the rise of anti-Western Islamist movements, which have either come to power outright in some countries (Iran, Sudan, post–Soviet-era Afghanistan), or else exert a strong influence on government policy in others (Saudi Arabia, Pakistan). Many people mistakenly believe that most Muslims are Islamist, when in fact the Islamist movement is only a minority position. Perhaps the most important factor shaping the present wave of Islamophobia, though, is the extremely large and disproportionate media coverage given to Islamist-inspired terrorism, like the September 11 attacks, while relatively little media coverage is given to equivalent acts of terrorism by other groups or nation-states.

Contextual Factors

Islamophobia is heightened by a number of contextual factors. One of these is the fact that a high proportion of refugees and people seeking asylum are Muslims. Demonization of refugees is therefore frequently a coded attack on Muslims, for the words "Muslim," "asylum-seeker," "refugee," and "immigrant" become synonymous and interchangeable in the popular imagination. In this case, the common experiences of immigrant communities of unemployment, rejection, alienation, and violence have combined with Islamophobia to make integration particularly difficult.

This has led Muslim communities to suffer higher levels of unemployment, poor housing, poor health, and higher levels of racially motivated violence than other communities. For example, in 2003, when the Home Office produced a poster about alleged deceit and dishonesty amongst people seeking asylum, it chose to illustrate its concerns by focusing on someone with a Muslim name.[3] An end-of-year article in the *Sunday Times* magazine on "Inhumanity to Man" focused in four of its five examples on actions by Muslims.[4]

A second contextual factor is the skeptical, secular, and agnostic outlook with regard to religion that is expressed in the media, perhaps particularly the left-liberal media. The outlook is opposed to all religions, not only to Islam. Commenting on media treatment of the Church of England, the Archbishop of Canterbury remarked that the Church in the eyes of the media is "a kind of soap opera ... It is both ridiculous and fascinating."[5] Ridiculing religion by the media would appear to be even-handed, but since Muslims have less influence and less access to public platforms, attacks are far more undermining. Debates and disagreements about religion are legitimate in modern society and are, indeed, to be welcomed, but they need to take place on a symmetrical basis.

A third contextual factor is foreign policy in the UK and most Western countries, in general, regarding various conflict situations around the world. There is a widespread perception that the war on terror is in fact a war on Islam, and that the UK supports Israel against the Palestinians. In other conflicts, too, the UK government appears to side with non-Muslims against Muslims and to agree with the view that the terms "Muslim" and "terrorist" are synonymous. These perceptions of UK foreign policy may or may not be accurate. The point is that they help fashion the lens through which events are interpreted—not only by Muslims but by non-Muslims as well.

Negative Impacts

The cumulative effect of Islamophobia, exacerbated by the contextual factors mentioned above, is that Muslims are made to feel that they do not truly belong in their respective host countries—they feel that they are not accepted, let alone welcomed, as full members of society. On the contrary, they are seen as "an enemy within" or "a fifth column" and they feel that they are under constant siege.[6] In Britain, for example, a whole new generation of British Muslims is developing, feeling increasingly disaffected, alienated, and bitter.

A further negative impact of Islamophobia is that Muslim insights on ethical and social issues are not given an adequate hearing and are not seen as positive assets. "Groups such as Muslims in the West," writes an observer, "can be part of trans-cultural dialogues, domestic and global, that might make our societies live up to their promises of diversity and democracy. Such communities can ... facilitate communication and understanding in these fraught and destabilizing times."[7] But Islamophobia makes this potential all but impossible to realize.

"The most subtle and, for Muslims, perilous consequence of Islamophobic actions," a Muslim scholar has observed, "is the silencing of self-criticism and the slide into defending the indefensible. Muslims decline to be openly critical of fellow Muslims, their ideas, activities and rhetoric in mixed company, lest this be seen as giving aid and comfort to the extensive forces of condemnation. Brotherhood, fellow feeling, sisterhood are genuine and authentic reflexes of Islam. But Islam is supremely a critical, reasoning and ethical framework... [It] rather ought not to be manipulated into 'my fellow Muslim right or wrong'."[8] The writer goes on to add that Islamophobia provides "the perfect rationale for modern Muslims to become reactive, addicted to a culture of complaint and blame that serves only to increase the powerlessness, impotence and frustration of being a Muslim."[9]

Open and Closed Views

Race equality organizations and activists over many years have failed to include Islamophobia in their programs and campaigns. For instance, why did the Race Relations Amendment Act fail to refer to anti-Muslim prejudice? In order to begin to answer this question, it is useful to draw a key distinction between *closed* views of Islam, on the one hand, and *open* views, on the other. Phobic dread of Islam is the recurring characteristic of closed views. Legitimate disagreement and criticism, as well as appreciation and respect, are aspects of open views.

Whether Islam is seen as monolithic and static, or as diverse and dynamic

Closed views typically picture Islam as undifferentiated, static and monolithic, and as intolerant of internal pluralism and deliberation. They are therefore insensitive to significant differences and variations within the world of Islam and, in particular, they are unable to appreciate the existence of tensions and disagreements amongst Muslims. For example, they ignore debates about human rights and freedom in Muslim countries and contexts, about appropriate relationships between Islam and other world faiths, and between Islam and secularism. In short, debates and differences which are taken for granted amongst non-Muslims are neither seen nor heard when they take place within Islam.

Sweeping generalizations are then made about all Muslims, in ways which would not happen in the case of, for example, all Roman Catholics, or all Germans, or all Londoners. Also, it is all too easy to argue from the particular to the general in the case of Muslims—any episode in which an individual Muslim is judged to have behaved badly is used as an illustrative example to condemn all Muslims without exception.

Diversity within Islam, like diversity within other religions, is multi-faceted and multi-dimensional. Some of the differences that tend to be ignored or over-simplified in much Islamophobic discourse pertain to those between Muslims of various countries, such as between the Middle East and South Asia, or Iranians and Arabs. Other examples include the difference between Muslims who are profoundly critical of the human rights records of certain Muslim countries and those who maintain that such criticism is merely a symptom of Islamophobia. Other differences that tend to be overlooked are the ones found between the perceptions and experiences of women and men, or the older and younger generations, particularly in the Muslim communities of Western Europe; or the ones between members of different social classes or the wide range of political movements and parties. Another important difference is that between the diverse interpretations of terminologies, doctrines and injunctions in the Qur'an and Islamic traditions, and between major strands and paths in the twentieth century, such as Sufism and Islamism, or movements known as modernism and revivalism.

A recurring word in the Western media nowadays is "fundamentalism." This is not a helpful term. It was coined as self-definition by a strand within Christianity and only much later, almost as a metaphor, applied to criticize aspects of Islam. It is emphatically not a term which Muslims themselves ever use for purposes of self-definition, and the "fundamentals" in Islam to which it claims to refer are of a different order from those to which it refers in Christianity.[10]

Whether Islam is seen as other and separate,
or as similar and interdependent

Closed views see a total difference between Islam, on the one hand, and the non-Muslim world, particularly the so-called West, on the other. Islam is the "other," with few or no similarities between itself and other civilizations and cultures, and with few or no shared concepts and moral values. Further, Islam is seen as hermetically sealed off from the rest of the world, with no common roots and no borrowing or mixing in either direction.

The alternative, "open" view sees similarities and shared values, as well as shared problems and weaknesses, and many kinds of interaction. In the open view it is impossible to assert that, for example, Islam is "East" and Europe is "West" (or Judeo-Christian), with no interconnections or commonalities. On the contrary, the open view stresses that there are close links between the three Abrahamic religions. At the same time it acknowledges that there are significant differences between Islam, Christianity, and Judaism, and that each has its own specific outlook on what these differences are, and on how they should be managed.

Whether Islam is seen as inferior, or as different but equal

Claims that Islam is different and "other" often involve stereotypes and views about "us" (non-Muslims) and "them" (Muslims), and the notion that "we" are superior, civilized, reasonable, generous, efficient, sophisticated, enlightened, and non-sexist. "They" are primitive, violent, irrational, scheming, disorganized, and oppressive. An open view rejects such simplistic approaches. It acknowledges that Islam is different in significant respects from other religions and from the West, but does not see it as deficient or as less worthy.

A perception of the inferiority of Islam includes such examples as the belief that Muslim cultures mistreat women; that Muslims co-opt religious observance and beliefs to bolster or justify political and military projects; that they do not distinguish between universal religious tenets, on the one hand, and local cultural mores on the other; and that they are compliant, unreflective, and literalist in their interpretation of scriptures.

Whether Islam is seen as an aggressive enemy or as a cooperative partner

Closed views see Islam as violent and aggressive, firmly committed to barbaric terrorism, and implacably hostile to the non-Muslim world. Islam was once, said Peregrine Worsthorne in the early 1990s, "a great civilization worthy of being argued with, but now it has degenerated into a primitive enemy fit only to be sensitively subjugated."[11] Thus, Islam is perceived as a threat to global peace:

> Muslim fundamentalism is fast becoming the chief threat to global peace and security as well as a cause of national and local disturbance through terrorism. It is akin to the menace posed by Nazism and fascism in the 1930s and then by Communism in the 1950s.[12]

Whether Muslims are seen as manipulative or as sincere

Islam means "submission" (not "peace") and it is the aim of Muslims ("those who have submitted") to make the whole world submit. The teaching seems not to envisage the idea of Muslims as a minority, except as a temporary phenomenon. The best that non-Muslims—in Britain that means Sikhs and Hindus, as well as Jews and Christians—can hope for is that they be treated as *dhimmis*, second-class citizens within the Islamic state.

It is frequently alleged that Muslims use their religion for strategic, political and military advantage rather than as a religious faith and as a way of life shaped by a comprehensive legal tradition. The *Observer* article which first popularized the term "Muslim fundamentalism" asserted that Islam had been "revived by the ayatollahs and their admirers as a device, indistinguishable from a weapon, for running a modern state." Muslims are assumed to have an instrumental or manipulative view of their religion rather than to be sincere in their beliefs, for their faith is "indistinguishable from a weapon."[13]

Whether discriminatory behavior against
Muslims is defended or opposed

Islamophobia in Britain is often mixed with racism—violence and harassment on the streets, and direct or indirect discrimination in the workplace. A closed view of Islam has the effect of justifying such racism. The expression of a closed view in the media, for example, gives support and comfort to racist behavior. Islamophobia merges with crude color racism, since most Muslims are perceived to have black or brown skins, and also anti-immigrant prejudice, since Muslims in Britain are perceived to have alien customs, specifically Asian.

Whether anti–Muslim discourse is seen as natural or as problematic

The expression of anti-Muslim ideas and sentiments is getting increasingly acceptable. They are natural, taken-for-granted ingredients of the everyday world of millions of people.

It is not only the tabloid newspapers that demonize Islam. There are routine derogatory references in all the press, in pamphlets and books. Even organizations and individuals known for their liberalism and anti-racism express prejudice against Islam and Muslims. As one correspondent put it: "A deep dislike of Islam is not a new phenomenon in our society. What is new is the way it is articulated today by those sections of society who claim the mantle of secularism, liberalism and tolerance... They preach equality of opportunities for all, yet turn a blind eye to the fact that this society offers only unequal opportunities for Muslims."

How Can Islamophobia Be Fought?

To answer this we must examine its causes. Firstly, there is prejudice; unfortunately, education is not enough to dispel it. Secondly, there is the smear of terrorism. The third cause is ignorance, of which the *hijab* issue is a classic example. I wonder how far Muslims realize that non-Muslims have little understanding of Islamic distinctiveness. Only grassroots contact can combat this. I recently spoke in a mosque at a

Christian-Muslim "Meeting for Better Understanding." The priest and I presented the position of our respective religions on a specific topic, and these meetings have proved immensely helpful in building mutual understanding.

Finally, the fourth cause is the lack of democracy in the Muslim world. Here is the one issue where critics of Islam have a point. Most Muslim states are repressive and only a minority are genuine democracies. In addition, far too many non-Muslim minorities there are marginalized if not harassed. Even if the average Briton rarely darkens a chapel door, the traditional British sense of fair play will cause him to view negatively the denial of religious liberty and/or equality to non-Muslims, especially to Christians.

It is sad that some of the greatest enemies of Islam can be found in the dictators of Muslim countries. The best solution to the stagnation of the current Muslim *ummah* (global nation) and to Islamophobia itself is to apply true Islamic principles based on the Holy Qur'an and Hadith. According to the great Muslim thinker, Muhammed Qutub, the best way to counteract hostility to Islam and Muslims is through faith. A secular and non-religious approach will not solve the current crisis, but a solution can be found with new and brave ideas, regardless of their source, as long as they follow and adhere to Islamic principles.

Muslims need to rediscover the art of generosity. They should think of Islam as a garden. The thing about a garden is that all this truly monumental variety of life exits in symbiosis: nourishing each other and ensuring the overall survival of the garden. Of course the garden has to be tended: the weeds have to be cleared, plants have to be pruned, and we have to make sure that nothing over-grows—that is, no single interpretation becomes an overarching, totalitarian ideology so much so that it ends up suffocating and endangering other plants. It is not for nothing that the garden is the central metaphor of the Islamic paradise.[14]

Notes

1. There are examples in Allen and Nielsen (2002), and on the websites of the Forum Against Islamophobia and Racism, the Islamic Human Rights Commission and *The Muslim News*.
2. This particular insult was made by Denis MacShane MP, minister of state at the Foreign and Commonwealth Office, in November 2003. It was compounded by the feebleness of his apology a few days later.
3. *The Muslim Weekly*, 5-11 December 2003, p.11. The text on the poster read "Ali did not tell us his real name or his true nationality. He was arrested and sent to prison for 12 months." This statement was translated into five languages, all of them connected with Muslim countries. A detailed legal reference was given in small print, but, in fact, the case that was cited had nothing to do with asylum and nationality claims.
4. One of the five examples was about a legal case that was *sub judice* at the time. A British Muslim had been arrested and charged but not yet tried or convicted.
5. In an interview with Charles Moore at Lambeth Palace, Dr. Rowan Williams, the Archbishop of Canterbury, had this to say about Islam: "It's a religion whose primary focus and interest is about unity, the unity of God and the unity of the faithful community under God. That is one of the great Arabic words, *Tawhid*... And that integrating vision is a universal vision of a community under God... That is what has given Islam its moral power and passion through the centuries...."
6. The sense of being under siege is global, not confined to Britain: see Akbar S. Ahmed, *Islam under Siege: Living Dangerously in a Post-Honour World* (Cambridge: Polity Press, 2003).
7 Tariq Modood, "The Power of Dialogue," in Muslim Council of Britain, *The Quest for Sanity* (2002), pp. 112–116; and idem, "Muslims and the Politics of Multiculturalism in Britain," in Eric Hershberg and Kevin Moore, *Critical Views of September 11: Analyses from Around the World* (New York: The New Press, 2002), pp. 193–208.
8. Merryl Wyn Davies, "Willful Imaginings," *New Internationalist*, no. 345 (May 2002).
9. Ibid.
10. The term "fundamentalism" was coined as a proud self-definition by a movement within American Protestantism in the period 1865–1910. It became publicly well-known from 1919 onwards, with the foundation of the World Christian Fundamentalist Association. The movement stood for a re-affirmation of historic Christian theology, morality and interpretation of scripture—the so-called fundamentals—and was in opposition to modernizing and liberalizing tendencies in American church life. Its essential

distinguishing feature was an insistence on a literal interpretation of the Bible. Christian fundamentalism, both in its theological aspects and in its interaction with right-wing politics, continues to be considerably stronger in the United States than in Europe.

The term was first used about Islam in the *Middle East Journal* in 1957. But it was not until 1981 that its application to Islam gained currency in the wake of an article by Anthony Burgess in the *Observer* referring to "the phenomenon of the new, or rather very old, Islam, the dangerous fundamentalism revived by the ayatollahs and their admirers as a device, indistinguishable from a weapon, for running a modern state." When applied to Islam the term refers virtually always to political matters, not to theology, and more especially to the use of terror or repression. Because of its origins in Christian theology and disputation, particularly with regard to doctrines about the inerrancy of scripture, there is a tacit assumption in the Western media that the use of terror by dissidents or repressive states is sanctioned or even encouraged by the Qur'an.

11. The *Sunday Telegraph*, February 3, 1991.
12. Clare Hollingworth, *International Herald Tribune*, November 9, 1993.
13. See note 10.
14. Source "Cultivating the Soil" by Ziauddin Sardar, *Emel Magazine*, September 2000.

CHAPTER TWO

ISLAMOPHOBIA:
Meaning, Manifestations, Causes

Mustafa Abu Sway

"Muslims could change their world and overcome the tyranny of Islamophobia and anti-Muslim discrimination, just as slavery was abolished"[1]

Islamophobia consists of violence against Muslims in the form of physical assaults, verbal abuse, and the vandalizing of property, especially of Islamic institutions including mosques, Islamic schools, and Muslim cemeteries. Islamophobia also includes discrimination in employment, where Muslims are faced with unequal opportunities; discrimination in the provision of health services; exclusion from managerial positions and jobs of high responsibility; and exclusion from political and governmental posts. Ultimately, Islamophobia also comprises prejudice in the media, literature, and everyday conversation.[2]

Let us consider the following examples:

- A mosque in the French city of Carpentras in the Provence–Alpes–Côte d'Azur region came under Molotov cocktail attack on Friday, November 11, [2005] during the weekly Friday prayer.[3]

- Twelve drawings depicting Prophet Muhammad in different settings appeared in Denmark's largest circulation daily *Jyllands-Posten* on September 30, [2005]. In one of the drawings, Prophet Muhammad appeared with a turban shaped like a bomb strapped to his head.

- Police arrested two people, apparently a Jewish pimp and a prostitute, on the Friday night of August 26 [2005] on suspicion that they were responsible for a pig's head dressed in a *keffiyeh* and inscribed with the nickname "the Prophet Muhammad" being thrown into the yard of Tel Aviv's Hassan Beik Mosque.[4]

- The U.S. military detailed on Friday, June 3, 2005, five cases in which jailers at the U.S. prison in Guantanamo Bay, Cuba, had desecrated copies of the Holy Qur'an, including one incident that had occurred as recently as March. Brigadier General Jay Hood, commander of the Guantanamo prison who headed the inquiry, said the inquiry had confirmed five cases of desecration.

- "Did you hear about the Muslim virgin desperate to lose it? It wasn't really the sex she was interested in; she just didn't want to [f**k] a suicide bomber when she died." The British journalist Julie Burchill's "favorite joke of the moment," in "What Allah Wants, Allah Gets" as reprinted in the Israeli daily, *Haaretz* (September 24, 2005).

Who Are the Islamophobes?

The countries where these offensive and troubling Islamophobic examples took place are France, Denmark, Israel, and the U.S. Other examples in the article include Germany, Sri Lanka, and the UK. The list fails to reflect the fact that Islamophobic incidents exist in every country where there is a Muslim minority. Islamophobia-Watch.com has documented Islamophobic entries under the name of these additional countries: Australia, Austria, Belgium, Canada, Italy, the Netherlands, and Spain.

In addition, the perpetrators could be categorized as either individual civilians or officials, including military. There is a problem about determining the Islamophobe in the last example given above; is it only the author, Julie Burchill? How far could *Haaretz* itself be held responsible for the Islamophobic content? (The original responsibility, in this case, does not pertain to *Haaretz* but to Burchill herself and *The Times*. In both dailies, however, the piece was printed verbatim, without asterisks to replace the "f" word. The comments on the article were no less Islamophobic. The question here arises regarding *Haaretz*'s editorial choice.)

Seventy-Two Virgins?

Julie Burchill was reminded of the "joke" after she noted that "Palestinian cretins felt it entirely necessary to murder innocent Israelis in order to have an orgy in heaven with 72 virgins." While I can take issue with several points in this venomous statement, I would like to highlight the problem of the "72 virgins" construct and its place in the Islamic worldview. It is a matter of fact that the "72 virgins" construct does not exist either in the Qur'an or in the most authentic of the *Hadith* compendia.

As a person who attends the mosque on a regular basis and has listened to hundreds of Friday sermons, mostly at Al-Aqsa Mosque in Jerusalem, but also in the U.S., Europe, Africa, and South-East Asia, I cannot recall even one instance when this construct was mentioned in the mosque. The same applies to the Islamic academic institutions where I taught over the years. As it is in non-Islamic literature rather than in Islamic books that this construct appears, it prompted me to carry out some research regarding the topic. I tracked it to a book by a ninth-century Muslim scholar, Al-Tabarani, in his *Muʿjam*. The conclusion is that this construct does not form part of the Islamic faith, but tends to be often misused by Islamophobes for their twisted reasons.

Incidents on the Rise

The examples mentioned above depicting Islamophobia fail to show that Islamophobic incidents are on the rise. Statistics, however, indicate a two-hundred-percent rise in certain places in Europe. *The Times* notes that in France

> [t]he number of hate crimes, most notably against Jews and against Arabs of North African origin, nearly doubled last year, to 1,565 from 833 a year earlier, according to a report to the government by the National Consultative Commission for Human Rights... Acts against people of North African origin totaled 595 in 2004, up from 232 in 2003.[5]

This rise could be attributed to the growing number of Islamophobes and Islamophobic institutions, and the normalization of hostility towards Islam. The ease with which information travels in the age of globalization takes the Islamophobic act from its local context to the international arena, thus creating an impression that there is a universal Islamophobic ethos that haunts Muslims.

By drawing attention to the above-mentioned examples, I simply hope that the reader will get a sense of the tragic state of Islamophobia. The content is offensive, not only to Muslims, but to any ethical person. The intensity with which Islamophobia is spreading not only poses a real danger to Muslim minorities, but also threatens the social fabric wherever they live.

Individual versus Institutionalized

The perpetrators range from Islamophobic individuals acting "on their own" to institutionalized Islamophobic policies. But, are individual Islamophobes really "on their own"? The answer is, in one sense, Yes. As long as they are not fulfilling governmental orders or institutional plans, then they are "on their own." On the other hand, those individuals are bombarded by the biased media, which are yoked to the centers of power, with stereotypical images of Muslims; they listen to right-wing, xenophobic politicians who reinforce those stereotypes and call for the expulsion of Muslims, and they read post–Cold War scenarios that portray Islam as the new enemy that replaced Communism—the green menace in place of the red. The list of possible influences could include school curricula and exclusivist theological worldviews that neither accommodate nor engage the "other." Sometimes the line between individual and institutional Islamophobia gets blurred. The following example might clarify the point: Forty-eight-year-old Kamal Raza Butt, a Pakistani man who is visiting friends and family in Nottingham [UK], is set upon by a gang of white youths. He is allegedly called "Taliban" and then punched to the ground and later dies in hospital. Two 16-year-old youths are charged with manslaughter, seven others are freed on bail pending further inquiries.[6]

Did the mob act on the spur of the moment? The incident is presented in the media without questioning the motives. The wider context within which the role of the UK in Afghanistan and Iraq, the July 7 attacks in London, and the attack in Nottingham could be seen as interconnected was not addressed. What motivated the Nottingham attack remains unclear. One thing is certain: if the roots of Islamophobia are not addressed, the problem will persist.

Institutionalized Islamophobia, on the other hand, reflects governmental laws or policies. As an example let us consider the case of extreme secularism in France. It was used to pave the road for an Islamophobic law[7] which prohibits the display of religious symbols, effectively targeting and banning the wearing of headscarves by Muslim schoolgirls. If one accepts the right to display crosses and yarmulkes while denying a Muslim girl the right to wear her *hijab* (headscarf), then this position is Islamophobic. It reflects the inability of France to celebrate multiculturalism and to see Islam as a positive force that could contribute to the welfare of the society. Rather than accommodating its own Muslim citizens and integrating them into the society according to a multicultural paradigm for coexistence, France opted for an extreme and fundamentalist notion of secularism—proof of a loss of the French ethos that once was based on *liberté, égalité, fraternité* (liberty, equality, fraternity).

The Case of the *Hijab*

Islamophobic policies target the *hijab* as a symbol of Islam. The specific government that adopts the banning of the *hijab* reflects deep-seated antagonism toward Islam. The sad fact is that many countries are following suit. In Germany, the ban on *hijab* is slated to take effect in August 2006. "Female and male teachers are not allowed to express any worldviews or any religious beliefs which could disturb or endanger the peace at school ... That's why we want to forbid [female] Muslim teachers at state schools from wearing headscarves," said North Rhine–Westphalia schools minister Barbara Sommer.[8]

The ban on *hijab* has also spread to South Asia, where two Muslim teachers were suspended from their work at a government school in Badulla in north-east Sri Lanka earlier this year because they wear the *hijab*. In addition, S. Satchchitanandan, the provincial minister for Tamil education, ordered that the government-run school be renamed the Hindu Girls School—the Tamils are predominantly Hindus, while the Sinhalese are Budhhists. The school has more than 200 Muslim girl students.[9]

It is virtually impossible to narrate all the distressing incidents involving the *hijab*, but if I had the chance to add a picture of a woman with her head covered to help the reader understand the Islamophobic nature of the ban of *hijab*, I would have used that of the late Mother Theresa, the Roman Catholic nun and founder of the Sisters of Charity. She was modestly dressed with her head covered with a headdress, a *hijab* if you will!

Pseudo–Political Correctness, Pseudo-Scholars

Another type of institutional negative role is the constitutional and legal structures behind which Islamophobes can hide. Attacking Islam and Muslims takes place in the name of the freedom of expression, which is protected by the First Amendment in the United States. This legal structure allows Islamophobic institutions and neo-con pundits who are driven by an irrational fear of Islam and Muslims to malign Muslim leaders and to smear mainstream Muslim organizations. At times, it is calculated Islamophobic statements that are systematically stated in some U.S. media to keep the society polarized and to prevent Muslims from being at home in their own countries. When some right-wing Christian preachers like Jerry Falwell, Billy Graham, and Pat Robertson made defamatory statements about Islam,[10] none of them was held accountable; it is not possible to try them and win according to U.S. law.

One can contrast this with what happened to their Evangelical colleagues in another part of the world. A state tribunal in Australia [Dec. 17, 2004] found two Evangelical Christian pastors who conducted a church seminar on Islam guilty of inciting hatred against Muslims. Daniel Nalliah and Daniel Scott of Catch the Fire Ministries were tried under Victoria's new race and religion hate laws after the Islamic Council of Victoria filed legal action, charging Scott called Muslims demons, liars, and terrorists.[11]

This trial is good news; people of conscience should help create race and religion hate laws in all countries. An alliance between the various communities is needed to combat all forms of hate crimes, including Islamophobia, which should be criminalized.

In addition, the vilification of Muslims takes place at the hand of pseudo-scholars of Islam who abuse the freedom that the First Amendment grants them. A good example is the case of Daniel Pipes. He began a recent article, "Islamophobia?" in the *New York Sun* (October 25, 2005), with the following statement:

> An Islamist group named Hizb-ut-Tahrir seeks to bring the world under Islamic law and advocates suicide attacks against Israelis. Facing proscription in Great Britain, it

opened a clandestine front operation at British universities called "Stop Islamophobia."[12]

Any true scholar of Islamic movements knows that Hizb-ut-Tahrir never advocated suicide attacks against anyone; they are strictly speaking a political movement. They are criticized for their aggressiveness in promoting their political views and—yes—they are criticized for not participating in resisting the Israeli occupation. They do call for the reinstitution of the Caliphate (i.e. a pan-Islamic polity) system that existed until 1924, a matter which should be left entirely to Muslims to sort out amongst themselves. To outlaw Hizb-ut-Tahrir in Britain would be a clear Islamophobic act and a true violation of the freedom of expression.

Such Islamophobic pseudo-scholars hide behind politically correct statements to the effect that they do not have a problem with moderate Islam, or with moderate Muslim intellectuals. This was an argument Pipes used on al-Jazeerah TV channel's *Open Forum* on May 28, 2005. When asked to mention one moderate Muslim, Pipes named two intellectuals, one from the Sudan and one from Egypt, both of them long dead. Is the message here that there are no moderate Muslims alive, or that moderate Islam is dead?

It is unfortunate that President Bush went on to nominate Pipes to the board of the renowned United States Institute of Peace, against the will of the Congress.

Islamophobia and the Palestinian Question

While the Palestinian people comprises Jews [Samaritans], Christians, and mostly Muslims, a consistently Islamophobic propaganda is being used against the Palestinian people to prevent them from ending the Israeli occupation.

One of the organizations that systematically use crude and vile Islamophobic statements is the Israel Hasbara Committee [an unofficial non-governmental organization]. Their website features hundreds of Islamophobic articles that aim ultimately at discrediting the Palestinians and their just cause. One of the Israel Hasbara Committee's featured writers, Michael Anbar, paints an Islamophobic picture of the Palestinian leadership, in which

> [t]he PLO follows an Islamist policy similar to al-Qaeda. Very much like bin Laden and the Iranian Ayatollahs, Yasser Arafat openly calls for Jihad against Israel and the West, a holy war that nominally obligates all Muslims worldwide to kill infidels, Jews in particular.[13]

In a different article, and in what seems to be a slip of the tongue, the Israel Hasbara Committee revealed its true character through the following statement:

> War is dirty, whether it is on the battlefield or in the propaganda world. It is time to use the weapon of relentless repetition.[14]

Only enemies of peace would continue to be against an end to the Israeli occupation. To be against the establishment of a Palestinian state could be described as an essentially Islamophobic position.

Concluding Remarks

Though the Islamophobic examples used in this article are contemporary, Islamophobia itself is not new. The Crusades and, later on, the Inquisition in Spain reflect a very problematic historical relationship with Jews and Muslims. The Catholic Church in its *Nostra Aetate*[15] has called for tolerance and fellowship among peoples of all faiths. How much of the old hatred has it been able to eradicate as it celebrates its fortieth year?

As with the advent of any new terminology that describes a specific phenomenon, it takes time to connect both. The phenomenon that Islamophobia describes is not uncommon, and is as old as Islam itself. The case of Islamophobia is just like that of anti-Semitism,[16] where discrimination against and the persecution of the Jews took place for many centuries before the term "anti-Semitism" was coined.

I would argue that Islamophobia and anti-Semitism are rooted in xenophobic Eurocentrism which was and still is a barrier to fostering a multicultural world not dominated by nationalism and national interests. Other paradigms should replace the existing world order which has already caused so much destruction at the turn of the twenty-first century in Islamic lands.

I would like to conclude by quoting excerpts from UN Secretary-General Kofi Annan's address to the Department of Public Information (DPI) seminar, "Confronting Islamophobia: Education for Tolerance and Understanding," in New York, December 7, 2004:

> An honest look at Islamophobia must also acknowledge the policy context. The historical experience of Muslims includes colonialism and domination by the West, either direct or indirect. Resentment is fed by the unresolved conflicts in the Middle East, by the situation in Chechnya, and by atrocities committed against Muslims in the former Yugoslavia. The reaction to such events can be visceral, bringing an almost personal sense of affront. But we should remember that these are political reactions—disagreements with specific policies. All too often, they are mistaken for an Islamic reaction against Western values, sparking an anti-Islamic backlash…

> …[I]slamophobia is at once a deeply personal issue for Muslims, a matter of great importance to anyone concerned about upholding universal values, and a question with implications for international harmony and peace. We should not underestimate the resentment and sense of injustice felt by members of one of the world's great religions, cultures and civilizations. And we must make the re-establishment of trust among people of different faiths and cultures our highest priority. Otherwise, discrimination will continue to taint many innocent lives, and distrust might make it impossible to move ahead with our ambitious international agenda of peace, security and development.[17]

Notes

1. http://www.blink.org.uk/pdescription.asp?key=9255&grp=30&cat=138 Reported on 19/9/2005 (Shirin Aguiar-Holloway, in "Islamaphobia [sic] is New Slavery," paraphrasing Hamza Yusuf's statement to a gathering of Muslim representatives at the House of Lords in the UK.)
2. http://www.runnymedetrust.org/publications/pdfs/islamophobia.pdf
3. http://www.islamonline.net/English/News/2005-11/12/article02.shtml
4. http://web.israelinsider.com/Articles/Briefs/6408.htm (August 27, 2005)
5. http://www.trans-int.com/quarterly (quoted in John Rosenthal, "Beyond the Numbers Games: A Closer Look at the Statistics on Anti-Semitism and 'Islamophobia' in France")
6. http://news.bbc.co.uk/2/hi/uk_news/england/nottinghamshire/4680891. stm 10 July 2005
7. Law 2004-228 of March 15, 2004, signed by President Jacque Chirac.
8. http://www.islam-online.net/English/News/2005-08/31/article01.shtml
9. http://www.muslimedia.com/archives/world99/sri-hijab.htm
10. http://www.islamonline.net/English/News/2002-11/26/article70.shtml
11. http://www.worldnetdaily.com/ Posted Dec. 18, 2004.
12. http://www.danielpipes.org/article/3075
13. http://www.infoisrael.net/cgi-local/text.pl?source=4/b/i/archives/ 281220032 (Dec. 15, 2003)
14. http://www.infoisrael.net/cgi-local/text.pl?source=4/b/viii/archives/ 140920051
15. Declaration on the relationship of the Church to non-Christian religions NOSTRA AETATE.was proclaimed by POPE PAUL VI. on October 28, 1965
16. Semites originally meant the descendents of Shem (Arabic=Sam), comprising Arabs (including Arab Christians and Muslims), and other Semitic peoples as well. Now, the term is used mainly to refer to Jews (i.e. Judeophobic or anti-Judaism). "New Anti-Semitism", on the other hand, refers to criticism of the State of Israel, which is portrayed as the ultimate Jew. This category could be used to silence legitimate criticism. Israel is a country that occupies other lands and other peoples; this results in direct violations of basic human rights. Israel also faces the choice of either being Jewish or democratic; so far Israeli laws have discriminated systematically against its non-Jewish citizens. Would such description fall under new anti-Semitism?
17. http://www.un.org/News/Press/docs/2004/sgsm9637.doc.htm

CHAPTER THREE

AN EAST-WEST DICHOTOMY
Islamophobia

Eugenio Chahuán

The September 11 attacks set into motion a profound and sensitive debate as the world realized that even the greatest power in the world can be vulnerable. The impact was felt far and wide, and Islam became the focus of attention in the media, in seminars, in forums, and in thousands of publications worldwide. Against the expectation of the many, religion does not seem to be on the wane; if at all, it is seeing a resurgence, coupled with an enormous capacity to mobilize and produce changes in various part of the world. There are the cases of Iran, the Philippines, Afghanistan, Palestine, Saudi Arabia, Ireland, the Balkans, Chechnya, and the U.S.A.—with Bush's born-again Christianity.

Today, most political leaders are adopting an apocalyptic discourse. They talk of the struggle against evil; they speak in the name of God and try to impose their own laws and their perception of the good. The

German philosopher and sociologist, Jürgen Habermas, pointed out in a conference that the September 11 attacks have led, in various ways, to the explosion of the tension between secular and religious societies. And the anticipation by some social analysts that the twenty-first century would start under the sign of a clash of religions, cultures, and civilizations seems to be materializing.

The Need for an Antithesis

The long-standing negative mental construct the West has of Islam and the Arabs has been intensified by the determining role played by the media these days, especially when they are in the service of colonial interests, military and economic expansionist ideologies, or a vehicle for the promotion of Western values, which necessarily calls for the demonization of the Other. This situation has been heightened in the wake of the collapse of the East-West system. It was a decisive turning point in the process of self-legitimization of the West which predicated its own identity upon an antithesis—Us/We as opposed to the Other/Them. The Gulf war (1991) that was orchestrated with a great deal of propaganda has since been used to breach the gap that was left by the unraveling of the Soviet bloc, replacing it by an even more radical one—Islam—generally seen not only as an antithetical ideology, but as an all-encompassing cultural antithesis to the West and its universal identity. In this sense Islam gets converted into the basis of anti-Westernism, anti-modernism, and anti-civilization all in one.

The psychological necessity of the Us to create its identity through the confrontation with and the discrimination against the Other serves, in this case, a dual purpose. On the one hand, it promotes the chauvinistic, xenophobic propaganda against the Orient, Islam, the Arabs, as well as many others; on the other hand, Islam is presented as a threat to the security of the West. In creating the new antagonism East-West, rationality-irrationality, modernity-traditionalism by pitting the Us against the Other, the West is in reality negating the fact that it has **since long** been **an** authentically multicultural **society**. The danger of the present cultural discourse against Islam is that it is in essence a racist discourse that lumps together without distinction **all persons of differing traits.**

The counterpoint is that such discrimination engenders a re-identification on the other side. By this is meant that the propagation of this erroneous dichotomy could serve dangerously as a self-fulfilling prophecy—those who perceive themselves as marginalized and are labeled as the new face of the enemy could be drawn into reconstructing their identity accordingly.

Mirror Constructs

Occidental societies have formed a distorted perception of the Arab world. Fanaticism, terrorism, and the danger of an immigration invasion are features attributed to the Arabs and the Muslims, while the qualities and the rich cultural and scientific heritage of these people and their contribution to civilization are being ignored. The problem of Islamophobia is very acute in countries like the U.S., and in many European countries where attacks have been carried out against Muslims for the simple fact that they are Muslims, as representatives of this Other that is not accepted on their own territory.

A mirror construct is happening on the side of the Other that finds itself totally invaded by the West in all areas of life. The Arab East has its own perception of the occidental Other. They are different images, even contradictory to the extent that each has formed his/her specific concept of the Occident and the Other. For the West, the Orient can be many things, springing from the divergence of interests and/or cultural and political assessments. For some, it is a place of exoticism, a haven of spiritual peace to flee the tumult of civilization. For others it can be a place for exploitation, colonialism, and domination; or the breeding ground of despotism, fanaticism, and fundamentalism. A similar disparity in perception is to be found in the East. To some, the West is a civilizing and political model that is to be imitated in order to emerge from a state of underdevelopment. It is also a font of scientific and cognitive knowledge that leads to liberation from the hold of traditionalism and fundamentalism. At the same time, the West also embodies the colonialist power as it sets out to subjugate the Muslim and the Arab, disparaging their values and exploiting their resources.

No More 'Mare Nostrum'

It has been argued by some, most notably by Edward Said, that the denigration of Islamic civilization associated with Islamophobia is central to the concept of Western civilization.

The ousting and marginalizing of Islam marks the **debut** of Western civilization and, thus, explains the depth and longevity of Western Islamophobia. In order to understand the Western vision of the Orient, it is necessary to go back in history. Christian Europe between the seventh and tenth centuries was shaken to its depths by the repercussions of the Arab Islamic conquests. From this moment onwards, the Orient became identified with Islam. Its birth and rapid expansion modified to a large extent the political geography of the Mediterranean basin. The Mediterranean Sea ceased to be *Mare Nostrum* ("our sea") and got converted into a place of confrontation between East and West. The Belgian historian and orientalist, Henri Pirenne, wrote in 1935, "Along the shores of Mare Nostrum since then lay two different and hostile civilizations."[1]

There were, then, two different worlds, two rivals who, since the outset, began their interactions on a belligerent footing. The Muslim Arab conquests were perceived as unjustified. The West was led into a defensive stance expressed in the denigration or the demonization of the aggressor; thus, the Muslim was termed as "devastator of cities," "destroyer," "hostage taker," or "white slave dealer."

> Islam was a provocation in many ways. It lay uneasily close to Christianity, geographically and culturally. It drew on the Judeo-Hellenic traditions. It borrowed creatively from Christianity—it could boast unrivalled military and political successes. Nor was this all. The Islamic lands sit adjacent to and even on top of the biblical lands. Moreover, the heart of the Islamic domain has always been the region closest to Europe.... From the end of the seventh century to the sixteenth century, Islam in either its Arab, Ottoman, North African or Spanish form dominated or effectively threatened European Christianity.[2]

From the Military to the Religious

The East-West confrontation that took place as a result of the Arab expansion in the eighth century was mostly political, economic, and cultural. The conflict between Christianity and Islam did not yet exist. This was to occur later with the Crusades between the eleventh and thirteenth centuries. Since then the Moor is no more the military enemy of the West, but Islam is the enemy of Christianity. With the Crusades the virtual line between the Christian West and the Muslim East is drawn and does not disappear except on rare occasions. To the negative image of the Muslim is added a pejorative view of Islam the religion. Such an image was so extensively promoted throughout the Middle Ages that it now forms part of the Western collective subconscious.

Starting with the thirteenth century, the Orient began to lose some of its glory. The Muslim Arabs were eclipsed by the emerging Ottoman Empire. The changes henceforth determine the Western perspectives of the East. If the religious antagonism lost its edge, it did not disappear entirely, as Islam through the Turk became the impetus behind the many voyages to the Orient. The main purpose was, nonetheless, to reaffirm the intellectual supremacy of the West and its art of governance, so much so that the basis of conflict between the two worlds ceased to be religious as much as political and cultural.

With the seventeenth to eighteenth centuries, the sense of superiority in the West gets coupled with technological progress. To the vital and progressive Europe is opposed the archaic and immobile East. The colonial act is thus seen as fully justified. In his *Philosophy of History*, Hegel incorporates this modern-primitive dichotomy, associating Islam and the Orient with the primitive world. Perhaps the most representative synthesis of the modern view of the East and Islam can be found in one of the discourses the French philologist and Orientalist Ernest Renan made at the Sorbonne in 1883, when he said that "Islam and the Muslim are incompatible with rationality."[3]

Intolerance and Mental Inertia

This Orientalist position is based then on a reality underpinned by the superiority of the Western Us over the foreign, i.e., the Orient, Them. Its tenet is the binary opposition of two worlds, two styles, and two cultures. It is the dichotomy between, on the one hand, the Westerners who are rational, pacific, liberal, logical, and capable of entertaining real values, and, on the other hand, the Orientals who possess none of these values. The confluence of negative images facilitates the triumph of the racist message of the ultra-right in the U.S.A. and Europe. The lack of respect towards other cultures and the exaltation of the Western model constitute a clear expression of intolerance and resistance to dialogue. Thus, nothing is more legitimate than for the West to exercise a benevolent tutelage over these weak people—spreading democracy and "our way of life."

This stereotyping is generated not only by a certain mental inertia to appreciate anything different, but also accomplishes an actively defensive function: the prejudices of today preserve and perpetuate the falsehoods of the past. The European colonial aggression in the Arab countries during the nineteenth and twentieth centuries has been justified by a series of arguments whose common denominator was the depreciation of the Other, and the negative view of the Arab today is an extension of the imperialist attitudes of a past not so far away,

The crises experienced by Arab societies today—economic, political, and cultural—run very deep and their solution is very complex. The violence, consequence of an accumulation of unresolved conflicts, cannot in any way be attributed to cultural or religious causes, and even less to a so-called genetic disposition towards fanaticism making up the identity of the Arab. This notion of identity dynamics has been conveniently and indiscriminately used, often leading to confused and inadequate analyses of the many conflicts in the Middle East, and giving rise to a monolithic view of the Arabs and the Muslims among the political community, the media, and even in the world of academe.

Conclusion

Undeniably, Islamism is gaining ground today. But this could be viewed as a result of decades of exploitation, political frustration, and discrimination. And this is what gives the Islamist movements their impetus. If the problems of today stem from a social origin and are getting reinforced by current economic and political processes, then their solution should be social, carried out on a genuinely transnational level through a policy of cooperation, especially in the economic sphere, and a sincere and balanced collaboration in the political domain. If the West is as rational as it claims, it should address the problems rationally and not through inadequate and inhumane means, such as armies and bombs.

Juan Goytisolo, the contemporary Spanish writer, has this to say about the situation: "The historical circumstances of the past forty years, the struggle against Western colonialism, the establishment of the State of Israel and the consequent expulsion of the Palestinians, the Lebanese civil war, and the Iranian revolution have all engendered situations of violence which place the Islamic world in bloc in the bench of the accused, as causing all the problems and ills that afflict the world. The Westerners seem to forget that their history and recent past does not qualify them to give lessons to anybody. Those who systematically denigrate Islam should be reminded that in this context there have never been bloody inquisitions such as ours, nor genocides of entire peoples such as those of the Amerindians and the Aborigines, nor the collective extermination of an entire people of the magnitude of Hitler's Holocaust, nor the use of lethal weapons as in Hiroshima and Nagasaki."[4]

Notes

1. Henri Pirenne, *Mahoma y Carlomagno*. Alianza Editorial, S.A., 1997 (Spanish).
2. Edward Said. *Orientalismo*. Madrid: Debate, 2002. (Spanish), p. 74.
3. Ernest Renan, as quoted in Edward Said, *Orientalismo* (Spanish), p.134.
4. Juan Goytisolo, *De la Ceca a la Meca*. Madrid: Alfagara, 1997. (Spanish).

CHAPTER FOUR

THE 'NEW ANTI-SEMITISM' AND THE MIDDLE EAST

Dina Porat

On July 2005, the media reported the brutal assault on two Yeshiva students in Kiev, perpetrated by a dozen skinheads. On the same day the newly elected pope, Benedictus XVI, gave a sermon in Cologne where, addressing an exceptionally large audience, he denounced the recent increase in anti-Semitism. Together, the two sides of this coin demonstrate today's dual and parallel processes—anti-Semitism and the response it evokes: the intensification of the various anti-Semitic expressions and the growing readiness of both Jewish and non-Jewish bodies to confront it.

Anti-Semitism has always been a product of problems and anxieties in given societies and periods of time. Yet with globalization, anti-Semitism has become increasingly connected not only to national or local societies but to the international arena as well.

Taking into consideration the claim that there is indeed a new anti-Semitism, starting as of late 2000, originating in circles and regions different from before, aiming at different targets, and using other verbal and visual tactics, the question to be asked is whether the image of the Jew has changed as well and, if it did, in what way? Second, are the current events in the Middle East the source of this new anti-Semitism, or are they the match that sets the fire but the woods lie elsewhere? Let us examine the relationship between Middle Eastern events and the anti-Semitism manifested in other regions of the world.

The New Anti-Semitism

The recent wave of anti-Semitic expressions that started in the late 1990s and intensified with the beginning of the second intifada was soon labeled the "New Anti-Semitism." It indeed has a number of new features: the main target has shifted from the desecration of cemeteries to the use of arson against synagogues, and to physical attacks against persons. This last development is both insulting and worrying, because most individuals who perpetrate it act sporadically and on the spur of the moment. Such channels of activity make it more difficult for the victims and the policemen to identify the perpetrators and bring them to justice.

The origin of violence has changed as well: the 1970s and 1980s witnessed activities of European extreme left and right, while the late 1990s brought about violence carried out mostly by young Muslims, either immigrants or second-generation newcomers to Europe. The extreme right is still active, though in a different format, more loosely organized in "leaderless cells." Thus like the young Muslims, they are harder to follow and catch. Another disturbing development is the growth in contacts between radical Muslim circles and the extreme right regarding anti-Semitism, though ideologically and ethnically they are in sharp dispute—the far right opposes open-door immigration policies and dreams about a homogeneous white Christian society. Verbal, visual, and digital expressions of anti-Semitism and stereotypes originate in local societies, academic circles, media, administration, and public opinion . Yet Muslim violence and local expressions cannot be dealt with separately. They feed on each other, since verbal expressions, especially those coming from or financed by Arab and Muslim countries, create a permissive atmosphere in which violence thrives and goes mostly unidentified and unpunished. Violence escalates the norms of hostility that the public accepts and grows accustomed to.

The geographic and political focus has shifted as well. The Soviet Union, which orchestrated, with the support of Arab and Third World countries, the UN attack on Zionism as if it equals racism, has collapsed. The initiative for anti-Semitic and anti-Zionist activities is no longer part of governments' agenda. It comes from the field, or various fields, rather than from above. Black Africa and the Far East embrace mentalities, tribal and ethnic traditions, and agendas in which anti-Semitism plays no role. In Latin America few cases of violence have occurred, the most notable ones being the two explosions in the Israeli Embassy and the Jewish community buildings in Buenos Aires. Eastern European and former Soviet Union countries have their own reasons for a low level of anti-Semitic activity: their poor economy does not attract immigrants, either Muslims or others; their ticket for a much-desired entry into the EU or NATO and other international and, especially, European organizations, is the proper keeping of a high level of human rights. "We are part of Europe," declared the young new Ukrainian president. Many in these Eastern European administrations are convinced—a deeply rooted anti-Semitic perception in itself—that the road to the wealthy pockets of Uncle Sam passes through alleged Jewish influence in the U.S.A. Unlike Western Europe, they are not undergoing a phase of post-colonialism or post-nationalism. Recently, after decades of Soviet indoctrination, they have discovered the Holocaust and their active part in it; and, finally, after decades of long and brutal deprivation of human rights, they are not easily impressed with similar accusations against Israel and its Jewish supporters. Still there is now increasing violence and virulent propaganda against Jews in Russia and the Ukraine. And it remains to be seen if and when the level of anti-Semitism will change in the ten countries newly accepted into the EU.

The centers of today's anti-Semitic expressions are Western Europe and North America, most notably France, Belgium, the UK, and Canada, followed to a lesser degree by Germany and the U.S. Here the shift is fully demonstrated—Western democracies rather than totalitarian or despotic regimes are producing anti-Semitism. This is a painful development, since democracies and their values have always been a beacon for Jews and for Zionism. The belief that these values are indeed equally applied to everyone was the basis for the hope Jews nourished to become a people accepted in the family of mankind, either as communities or as individuals, and a nation or a state equal to many other nations and states. Moreover, today it is mainly the European left, and not only the radical left, that fosters hostile attitudes towards Israel, often expressed in anti-Semitic and discriminatory terms. The Labor and leftist side of the Israeli and Jewish map find this development very hard to swallow, after a long history of Jewish initiative and innovation in leftist movements since the nineteenth century, and given the self-image of Israel as a socialist state in its first decades and a welfare state later.

This brings us to one more major characteristic of the "New Anti-Semitism." For the first time in the long history of anti-Semitism, which was born and fostered in Christian Europe, there is another major player in the arena—Middle Eastern Arab Islam. Radical Muslim propaganda deliberately blurs the distinction between anti-Semitism and anti-Zionism. The purpose behind this tactic is clear: the Arab world wages a war against the State of Israel. It uses old and even primitive motifs that European society is familiar with—Protocols of the Elders of Zion, blood libel, etc.—not against the Jews as individuals or communities but against the state. The result is also clear: the state in its entirety is portrayed as a Jewish state in a negative meaning, as a group bearing the characteristics allegedly portraying the Jewish people: cruelty, lust for blood and murder, treachery and greed, exploitation of manpower and resources, all in the service of the vile intention to dominate the world. The true nature of the relations between Israel and the Jewish communities abroad is completely twisted, and every form of anti-Semitism can be thus disguised as anti-Zionism. The very existence of a Jewish people is denied, and Zionism is accused of having invented it, much as other national movements invented their national identity, especially in the nineteenth century. Thus the clear alleged conclusion: such a state has no right to exist; moreover it is a constant danger to peace and stability in the world. Israel among the nations has become the Jew among people.

Anti-Zionism and Anti-Semitism

In the wake of this blurring of the picture, how can one know that anti-Zionism has crossed the lines and become anti-Semitism? First, let us distinguish between genuine criticism that refers to a given policy at a certain time and place and anti-Zionism. Then, let us first bear in mind that anti-Zionism, to the extent that it is directed against the very existence of Zionism as a national movement or against the existence of a state based on the Zionist idea or a Jewish people most of which supports it, is in any case discrimination against the Jewish people and an attempt to deny it the elementary right granted to every tiny island in the Pacific Ocean. And then let us turn to the following categories: anti-Zionism becomes anti-Semitism when the known classic anti-Semitic stereotypes keep being repeated and used in the vocabulary and the portrayal of images; when the hideous unforgivable comparison to the Nazi regime is brought up; when the Holocaust is distorted and turned into a political weapon, claiming it is used to blackmail economic or financial support, or denied and declared an invention of the wild cruel Jewish imagination; when the very right of the Jews to have a state is being undermined, and sometimes, though to a lesser extent, even their very existence as individuals or as a group; when criticism of Israel, and what are called its Jewish supporters, is out of proportion to reality or to criticism of other nations. This singling out reaches the absurd when Libya, Iran, Sudan, Saudi Arabia, for instance, complain about the violation of human rights, though it should be remembered that Israel, as a democracy, is judged according to higher standards; when the alleged character traits of the people are being projected on the state; and, finally, when the Jewish people and state are depicted as a cosmic source of all evil, from the fall of the Twin Towers to the death of Princess Diana, from the spreading of HIV to even the Tsunami—evil incarnate.

Not only Jewish or Israeli researchers and intellectuals bring up these criteria. The Webster's Third New International dictionary of 1966 defines anti-Semitism as hostility toward Jews and as "opposition to Zionism: sympathy with opponents of the state of Israel." A year later, Martin Luther King Jr. declared: "when people criticize Zionism, they mean Jews—this is God's own truth." And more recently, the report on European anti-Semitism published by Prof. Wolfgang Benz of the Berliner Technische Universitat and his team in 2003 stated most of the aforementioned parameters; a year later Romano Prodi, president of the EU commission, denounced "criticism against Israel, inspired by what seems to be anti-Semitic feelings and prejudices." President Bush's special envoy for anti-Semitism and Holocaust issues reached the same conclusions and published them on the last day of 2004; and during the sixtieth-year commemorations, standing in the snow of Auschwitz, Prof. Wladislaw Bartoszewski, former inmate of the camp and former Polish minister of foreign affairs, spoke about the cynical hiding of anti-Semitism behind anti-Zionism.

Summing up the answers to our first question regarding "New Anti-Semitism," today anti-Semitism is indeed expressed in new forms, arenas, and tactics, but it is using the same old and primitive motifs; and despite the exacerbation of the image of the Jew, its intensified condemnation and denunciation and the political use made of it, the image has remained basically the same.

The Role of the Middle East

The second question concerns the role of the Middle East in the increase of anti-Semitism. There is little doubt that the waves of violence against Jews are closely connected to the Israeli-Palestinian conflict, and the media bringing into every living room the picture of Israeli tanks confronting Palestinian youngsters further establishes the cruel image of an Israeli Jew. Taking a deeper look at the international political, social and economic scenes, one indeed realizes how they serve as a background for the anti-Semitic waves. They become fertile background when atmosphere correlates with Muslim interests, and administrations adopt policies that take into consideration oil resources and money, Muslim electoral capacity and UN voting.

The socioeconomic dimension is combined with the political one: European anti-Semitic motivation feeds on strong anti-American feelings, increased by the disintegration of the Eastern bloc which made the U.S. the strongest power in the world, allegedly disregarding Europe, "the Old World," as a factor in world politics. The U.S. is also the engine behind the globalization of the world economy, a process that created privatization and unemployment that has impoverished so many in the poor southern hemisphere and enriched the northern industrial rich countries. Globalization, which brought about the waves of immigrants flooding these countries, has created the most acute of today's problems, especially in Europe: the aging industrial countries need the cheap, unskilled working hands, but then they face multitudes that need healthcare, education, and civil rights that threaten the original cultures and traditions. The newcomers sharpen the inner disputes between the local parties regarding the duties of democracies, and strengthen the extremists on the right as well as on the left.

Anti-American feelings and anti-globalization movements serve as a meeting point with radical Islam that depicts the U.S. as the "Big Satan," the embodiment of the modern, cosmopolitan, industrial West, which runs counter to Islamic views. Israel, as a modern democratic state, is the "Small Satan," the Trojan horse that carries the West into the heart of the Muslim world. European leftists and radical Muslims connect the American domination with Jewish wealth, and the globalization with giant corporations, international money and Jewish magnates who ostensibly control the stock exchanges and the world markets. The Arab countries, mostly underdeveloped and destitute, looking for factors to blame for their situation, are the source of millions of immigrants—twenty million Muslim immigrants in Western and Central Europe by the end of 2004. The questions of the rights, status, and wages of the immigrants serve as a focal point of activity for hundreds of organizations, mostly non-governmental organizations (NGOs), involved in human-rights activity.

Let us try to portray one such activist: he or she is a staunch liberal, a pacifist, loathes every use of power, even if used for self-defense, as at least fascist; automatically justifies the underdog; struggles against economic exploitation; is definitely an anti-racist; s/he remembers with great pain and regrets the sins of European countries as colonialist powers; s/he dreams about a non-national world, about a united Europe devoid of the evils of nationalism. Thus, in today's atmosphere, s/he turns against Israel, depicting it as a last colonial outpost and as an unnecessary fulfillment of national desires, and against Jews at the forefront of

American power. He or she has more guilt feelings towards the millions of Muslims who have not integrated into the host societies than towards Jews in the wake of the Holocaust. He or she cannot express anxieties regarding growing Muslim influence or presence lest s/he be labeled a politically incorrect racist, and fosters a one-sided picture, in which s/he is bound to be only on the Arab-Palestinian side.

One more meeting point is the use of the memory of the Holocaust: the comparison of Israel to the Nazi regime is convenient to both Europeans and Palestinians. It minimizes the dimensions of the Holocaust, for it is clear even to those who make it that nothing of the kind is taking place, with gas chambers and mass annihilation. The comparison creates a kind of balance of account closing, between European countries which collaborated with the Nazis and the Jewish people. It can negate the right of the Jewish people to restore lost properties looted in the Holocaust, because Israel and its Jewish supporters have allegedly sinned as well. And, most importantly, it serves to reject Israel's legitimacy, for the Nazi regime had no right to exist, and neither does Israel.

Some Cautious Optimism

This brings us back to our starting point: anti-Semitism is on the rise and there are new responses to it. Those who carry out anti-Semitic activities and those who respond are different groups within the same countries, and the impact of recent responses of governments and organizations to the level of anti-Semitism is not yet felt. Let us entertain just a small amount of cautious optimism. Just as anti-Semitism is nourished by an array of international developments and interests, so is the reaction against it.

CHAPTER FIVE

WESTERN PERCEPTIONS OF ANTI-SEMITISM IN ARAB AND ISLAMIC DISCOURSE

Alexander Flores

In the past few years, anti-Semitism has once again become an issue. Jews and non-Jews alike claim that it is on the rise and the veracity of this assertion has by now become a bone of contention.[1] This anti-Semitism is seen to exist not only in Europe but on a global scale, and for many, the main realms of a rampant and vicious anti-Semitism are the Arab world, the Muslim diaspora in the West and, to a lesser extent, other parts of the Islamic world. Many of the perpetrators of violent acts against Jews in France during the year 2002 were, in fact, young male immigrants of Muslim (mainly Maghrebi) background. And a scrutiny of the content of Arab media reveals a certain amount of anti-Semitic statements. Outfits like the Middle East Media Research Institute (MEMRI), an institute that documents and translates Arab media items with a critical intention, remind us constantly of this fact.

The picture of Arab and Muslim anti-Semitism drawn in that context is horrifying. In many cases, it amounts to the claim that the Arabs are the true heirs of the Nazis. Whereas the open expression of anti-Semitism in the West is proscribed by virtue of the revelation of the Holocaust with all its horrors—so runs the argument—no such taboo exists in the Arab world. There, anti-Semitism was imported from Europe, became quite widespread, and survived its ostracism from the rest of the world.

Nazi Heirs?

In Germany, where the atmosphere is especially loaded because the specter of the Holocaust looms so large, some pieces along these lines can be found in a collection called *A New Anti-Semitism? A Global Debate*.[2] Jeffrey Herf's contribution "The New Totalitarian Challenge" is typical of the "alarmist" streak of the debate. According to him, we are witnessing a new wave of totalitarianism—the first one being the German and other European fascisms and Stalinism. This was overcome by the defeat of Nazi Germany and, later, the demise of the Soviet Union. Totalitarianism thus defeated in its traditional domain—Europe—was then transferred to the Arab and Islamic worlds, where it could grow and even become dominant, according to Herf. He points to certain roots of Arab-Islamic totalitarianism—French fascism, German national socialism, and Russian Stalinism—and sees it as composed of Arab nationalism in its Saddamist version and Islamic fundamentalism perceived as a vicious, anti-Semitic, and terrorist beast. "This wave that has taken root in the Arab and Islamic worlds consists of a mixture of secular Arab nationalism and Islamic fundamentalism. Added to that is an influence of French fascism, German national socialism, and Soviet communism that is tied up to secular pan-Arab radicalism and Islamic fundamentalism."[3]

Yet Herf's main contention is not with this totalitarianism but with the reaction of the European public to it. The world got rid of the "first wave" through vigilance and armed anti-fascism, and this experience should have been deeply engraved in the memory of European leftists and liberals. And indeed it was. But that changed. In the context of its sympathy for the anti-imperialist struggle of the Third World, the left developed an enmity towards the U.S. and Israel that was largely inspired by cultural anti-Americanism and anti-Semitism; that proved so persistent that it blinded its proponents to the dangers of the "new wave" of totalitarianism. Instead of coming out in full force against this threat and in unconditional support for the war against terror, spear-headed by the United States and the Israel of Sharon, they hesitated to hail the war in Afghanistan, came out vigorously against the war in Iraq, and found fault with Israel's oppression in the occupied territories. Needless to say, Herf supports that oppression ("Israel's justified retali-ation," p. 206) and those wars, again adducing the parallel with the war against Hitler, that might have been less costly and saved many millions of lives had it been waged in time as a preventive war—like the Iraq war. It is not always spelled out, but the implication is that the failure to identify Arab-Islamic totalitarianism is due to an anti-Jewish bias and, thus, to anti-Semitism even in Europe.

Typically, these warning cries concerning anti-Semitism in the Arab world are embedded in the picture of a new global anti-Semitism, and they are not accompanied by any precise depiction, let alone explana-tion, of the "oriental" anti-Semitism. Rather, it is taken for granted that it has the same character, scope, context, and possible effects as Nazi anti-Semitism. Some of the proponents of this view, like Herf himself, are historians of Nazi Germany but know next to nothing about the Arab or Islamic world. Accordingly, they refer extensively to Nazi anti-Semitism but detailed references to Arab or Islamic anti-Semitism are scarce, secondhand, or nonexistent. Such is the case with Omer Bar-tov, who also has a contribution in *The New Anti-Semitism* mentioned above. Apart from a number of what he alleges are instances of anti-Semitism in the West, he cites four occurrences that are supposed to demonstrate the dominance of a massive and vicious anti-Semitism in the whole Islamic world: the famous (or infamous) speech of former Malaysian Prime Minister Mahathir Mohammad at the summit of the Organization of the Islamic Conference (OIC) in November 2003; the murder of the American Jewish journalist, Daniel Pearl, in Pakistan;

some utterances by the perpetrators of September 11; and the charter of Hamas, the Palestinian Islamist organization.[4]

However revolting these instances are, they hardly serve to shed any light on the phenomenon of "Islamic anti-Semitism." Societies with Muslim majorities cover a large part of the globe; they differ vastly amongst themselves; they have huge discrepancies and contradictions within each of them; and they undergo varied experiences. In order to grasp any fact pertaining to these societies, one has to accurately describe it and to consider the given political and social juncture—mostly within a national framework and, only exceptionally, as in the case of the "free-floating" international terrorism, within a global one. And seen from that angle, the Mahathir speech, the murder of Daniel Pearl, the thoughts of Usama bin Laden and his ilk, and the Hamas ideology have vastly different backgrounds. To disregard this fact precludes any sound understanding of the phenomenon.

The Background

If these incidents have anything in common, it is the fact that they came against the background of an escalation of the Israeli-Palestinian conflict and large-scale and stepped-up Israeli oppression in the occupied territories. And it is precisely this common denominator about which our authors remain largely and curiously silent. To be sure, Bartov, for instance, denies the intention of mitigating Israel's occupation policies and warns us "never [to] confuse the legitimate criticism of Israeli policies with what all reasonable people agree is the despicable ideology of anti-Semitism."[5] Yet this is all he has to say about the subject.

This and similar pictures are quite widespread in Western perception. They shift the responsibility for the Palestine conflict and its existential character away from the realization of the Zionist project to which the Palestinians were reacting and onto a Palestinian anti-Semitism seen as an independent variable that led them to attack the Zionist enterprise, the latter being, thus, forced to defend itself to this very day. The ease with which this picture is accepted in leftist and liberal circles in Europe (and more specifically in Germany) is due to the perception of Zionism as a defensive reaction of Jews against mounting anti-Semitism in

Europe and the ensuing basic sympathy for Zionism and its product, the State of Israel—all this of course against one background: the horror of the Holocaust. That this defensive movement took the form of a colonizing one in the place where it achieved its realization, and caused enormous harm to the Palestinians, was less clearly and readily seen—helped by Israeli propaganda and widespread ignorance of facts and developments on the ground.

In the Arab world, it is the other way round. Everyday oppression in the occupied territories is perceived much more massively than in the West (most Arab TV stations have correspondents in Israel/Palestine), and, by and large, people are aware that this oppression does not come out of the blue, nor is it a mere defensive reaction against suicide bombers, but is the continuation of the century-old conflict. On the other hand, many of them do not see the defensive beginnings of Zionism in Europe because they are overwhelmed by its oppressive side in the Middle East. Seeing that the Holocaust is often brought forward to legitimize Zionism and Israeli actions and hence the Palestinians' predicament, many Arabs try to minimize its scope or even deny it altogether. Thus, the Holocaust deniers find receptive ears among Arabs. And what is at base sharp criticism and condemnation of Zionism and Israeli actions—quite justified considering the facts on the ground—all too often takes anti-Semitic forms insofar as no distinction is made between the Zionist movement (and, since its creation, the State of Israel) and world Jewry.

A Double Mix

As a consequence, there is a double mix: In the West, there is concern over the possible re-emergence of anti-Semitism and over the actual or alleged anti-Semitism one sees in the Arab and Islamic worlds. Against this background, Israel's actions in the occupied territories tend to be accepted as legitimate self-defense. This concern is used by an Israeli propaganda that portrays Arab enmity towards Israel as exclusively motivated by a deep-rooted and intense anti-Semitism of the Arabs. Inimical reaction to actual or potential anti-Jewish racism can take on the form of a general anti-Arab prejudice and, thus, another form of racism.

In the Arab world, on the other hand, there is sharp criticism of Israel and its actions, fed by these actions themselves, partly intermingled with an anti-Semitism that draws its inspiration from different sources: anti-Jewish themes of Islamic tradition, European anti-Semitism, resentment of the label "losers of modernization," and an Israeli leadership claiming that even its most brutal acts of oppression are in the best interest not only of Israel but of Jews worldwide.

The more these lines of argument are left entangled, the more they will reinforce each other and constitute a vicious circle. To break it, one has to separate the constituents of the respective mixtures. In the West, the rejection of Arab anti-Semitism should not prevent people from seeing Israeli injustice as an important background for the development of such anti-Semitism, and the latter should not be used to justify that injustice.[6] And regarding the Arab world, one should try to distinguish between conflict-induced enmity and anti-Semitism. Dan Diner, in a contribution to the German volume, states that the enmity of Palestinians and other Arabs towards Israel and Zionism is primarily due to the reality of the conflict, but that the origin of the anti-Jewish clichés and pictures through which this enmity is expressed should be sought elsewhere. One should seek them in the anti-Jewish elements of early Islamic tradition and, overwhelmingly, in traditional Christian anti-Judaism and modern "conspiracy-style" anti-Semitism that was borrowed from Europe. This has been readily accepted today, as it enables people to "understand" their marginal position in the world and their defeats more easily than by confronting the actual, complex causes. Conflict-induced enmity and anti-Semitic clichés have become so thoroughly intertwined that it gets virtually impossible to analytically disentangle them—or so Diner claims. Therefore, he suggests a "Gordian" approach: to fight anti-Semitism as if there were no Palestine conflict and to try to solve the conflict as if there were no anti-Semitism.[7]

This formula seems to imply that there is a contradiction between the two courses of action. This does not necessarily have to be the case. Arab anti-Semitism and the need to fight it do not stop us from trying to solve the conflict but are an additional incentive to do so. And work at a solution of the conflict is perfectly compatible with speaking out against Arab anti-Semitism. So let us try to do both. To do so, things have to get disentangled, and this is difficult as Diner rightly claims. One thing, however, has to be done, and that is a much more thorough analysis of Arab anti-Semitism than is available so far.[8] MEMRI, Robert Wistrich,[9] and others have drawn a distorted picture, for their own purposes. Many Arabs and others who resist the anti-Arab clichés have left the subject untouched because it appears embarrassing. Yet the problem exists, and it has to be tackled lest it become an additional stumbling block to the attempts to solve the problem on a rational and human basis.

Notes

1. See for instance the controversy around the study "Manifestations of anti-Semitism in the European Union" commissioned and, for a while, suppressed by the "European Monitoring Centre on Racism and Xenophobia."

2. *Neuer Antisemitismus? Eine globale Debatte*, edited by Doron Rabinovici, Ulrich Speck, and Natan Sznaider (Frankfurt: Suhrkamp, 2004). It should be noted that by no means do all contributions in this volume fall in the alarmist category

3. Jeffrey Herf, "Die neue totlitäre Herausforderung," in op. cit., pp. 191–210, here p. 195.

4. Omer Bartov, "Der alte und der neue Antisemitismus," in: op. cit, pp. 19–43, here pp. 33–43. A shorter version of this piece was published under the title "He Meant What He Said" in *The New Republic*, Feb. 2, 2004.

5. Bartov, 27.

6. Bartov is absolutely right when he states: "There is every reason in the world to reject attempts to justify objectionable Israeli policies by reference to the Holocaust" (Bartov, 27).

7. Ibid., 328s. The wording of the proposal takes up Ben-Gurion's famous formula from the beginning of the Second World War: To side with the British in the war against Nazi Germany as if there were no White Paper and to fight the White Paper as if there were no war

8. For a comparative review of two German monographs on the subject see, Alexander Flores, "Arabischer Antisemitismus zwischen Dämonisierung und Analyse," in: *Inamo* 37, spring 2004, 48-52.

9. The writings of Robert Wistrich are a main source for the proponents of the "Arabs Are Nazis" view; see e.g. his "Muslim Anti-Semitism: A Clear and Present Danger." (http://www.ajc.org/InTheMedia/PublicationsPrint.asp?did=503)

CHAPTER SIX

MIRROR IMAGES
Perception and Interest in the Israel/Palestine Conflict

John Bunzl

What is Anti-Semitism?

The frequency of verbal and sometimes physical attacks against Jews in Europe (particularly in France)—mostly in some way connected to developments in the Middle East—has led observers and interested commentators to declare the phenomenon of a "New Anti-Semitism." The Merriam-Webster International Dictionary (2004) even redefined the term "Anti-Semitism" in the following manner:

1. Hostility toward Jews as a religious or racial minority group, often accompanied by social, political or economic discrimination
2. Opposition to Zionism

3. Sympathy with opponents of Israel

The perception of (2) and (3) as anti-Semitic was promoted by the Israeli establishment, official Jewish communities, and American Jewish organizations.[1] The latter might have been additionally motivated (after 9/11) by a desire to present Israel and the Jews as victims of "international-Islamic terrorism." In contradistinction, one should remember that any meaningful definition of anti-Semitism follows number (1) mentioned above, i.e. hostility towards Jews as Jews, "because" they are Jews, irrespective of what they do or think. This would lead us to the conclusions that expressions of (2) and (3) could possibly only be constructed as anti-Semitic if and when they are directed against Israel because of the ascribed and stereotyped "Jewish" characteristics of this state.[2]

But what if hostility (at least in the Orient) is due to the perception of Israel as European, Western, alien, non-Arab, non-Islamic *and* particularly as repressive vis-à-vis the Palestinians? Don't we hear constantly that even attacks by Palestinians against Israelis are directed against them "*only* because they are Jewish"? Are there no other *reasons* for such acts, even if we condemn them? Is it so difficult, painful, and dangerous to look into these causes?

These difficulties result from the conflict itself.[3] We don't deal only with a confrontation between two peoples in one land but also with a process whereby one collective is brought in via migration and settlement while the other (native) collective is being replaced and repressed. Such a colonial process is in need of ideological justification. Therefore we find the interpretation of Arab resistance as groundless violence from the beginning of the Zionist enterprise, while one's own behavior is always constructed as counter-violence.

Islam and Anti-Semitism

So we have a conflict that is, structurally speaking, antagonistic "enough"—but due to its long duration and the needs of auto-justification, has become ideologized beyond recognition. In the Arab-Muslim world, hostility towards Israel, which defines itself as the state of the

Jews, is amalgamated with Judaeo-phobic images from Koranic sources and anti-Semitic stereotypes of Euro-Christian origin. Add to this a tendency to think in terms of conspiracy theories and a demonization of the West (beyond the real grievances) and you have a dangerous mix that has become part of the problem.

Looking into contemporary forms of Arab or Muslim hostility towards Israel and Jews, we have to state from the outset that they are to a large extent responses to a real conflict—and that they are and could be influenced in the future by its development. As in a mirror image,[4] hostility to Islam or Arabs in Israeli discourse does not stem from pre-existing trends in Jewish thought but from the conflict itself. "In principle" neither do Palestinians fight Israelis *because* they are Jews nor do Israelis fight Palestinians *because* they are Arabs.

But enemy images often have a life of their own; especially in conflicts of long duration combined with a continuous pressure for auto-justification and delegitimization of the "other." Often this is achieved by projecting the conflict deep into the past. Think of the grotesque exaggeration of the conflicts between the Prophet Mohammed and Jewish tribes in the seventh century by Islamist zealots.[5]

The Examples of Hizbullah and Hamas

Taking the examples of Hizbullah and Hamas, Esther Webman contextualizes the origins of Judaeo-phobic amalgams.[6] With Hizbullah she sees the negation of Israel as influenced by a combination of Khomeini's anti-Western orientation and negative images of Jews and Judaism in Islamic traditions. Other attitudes are derived from Christian-European sources: Jews/Zionists rule the world, the Torah commands Jews to kill; Jews control the media and—together with the Freemasons—strive for world domination, etc. On the other hand Israel is seen as a puppet of the U.S., perhaps a concession to the traditional Muslim imagination of Jews as weak and cowardly—in contradistinction to their image as powerful in the "Protocols of the Elders of Zion" (an anti-Semitic pamphlet originating in czarist Russia, still widely circulating in the Arab and Muslim worlds).

Obviously Hamas is more focused on Palestine, but in its ideological expressions the conflict is not seen as national or territorial, but as an opposition between Jews and Muslims, Judaism and Islam, falsehood and truth, infidels and believers. In addition, one can find references to European anti-Semitic fantasies: Jews were behind both world wars, they invented Communism, control the drug trade, manipulate the world economy, etc. As if in a mirror image of the Jewish settlement movement Gush Emunim's ideology of Greater Israel, the whole of Palestine is described as a *waqf* (Muslim endowment) which cannot be conceded in any form to infidels.

It would be wrong however to assume that Judaeo-phobic stereotypes *dominate* the discourse of Hizbullah or Hamas. Politico-tactical necessities or experiences with reality, pragmatic steps like prisoner exchanges, ceasefires (*hudna*) or the goal to participate in Palestinian Authority institutions, can modify "anti-Semitic" certainties.[7] And let's not forget that the image of the Jew in Palestinian society differs sharply from the European-Christian as well as from the traditional Islamic one because it is constantly amalgamated with the concept of "soldier," "settler," "Zionist," or "Israeli."

Arabs and the Holocaust

Traditionally, the Arabs saw the Holocaust as a European event. Europeans were responsible, and the Arabs should not "pay the price." The "price" usually was defined as the establishment and existence of the State of Israel at the expense of the Palestinians. This attitude cannot be attributed to anti-Semitism; its primary objective was to delegitimize the Zionist adversary. Arab attitudes should be seen within this perspective. There was no genuine treatment or research of this subject. Out of available positions—from denial via trivialization to justification—those fitting "best" to the respective needs and contexts were chosen.

The peace process of the 1990s and the mutual recognition between Israel and the Palestine Liberation Organization (PLO) offered an opportunity for parts of the Arab intelligentsia to deal with narratives of the "other" side. In this context, the centrality of the Holocaust for Israeli-Jewish self-understanding had to be recognized by Palestinian and

Arab intellectuals. The Holocaust entered Arab discourse and disputes not to legitimize the opposing collective but to better understand its complex motivations and their effects.[8]

Let's not forget that in spite of its drawbacks, Oslo had some positive impact on the awareness of at least elements of the Palestinian narrative in the Israeli public. It is not only due to the "New Historians" that concepts such as the "*nakbah*" (the Arabic word for catastrophe and the designation for "1948") became part of Israeli discourse. The trauma of the "other" became less taboo.

Arab "recognition" of the Holocaust was often undermined by putting this genocide and the *nakbah* on the same level—or by linking recognition of the European Jewish tragedy with demands for recognition of the *nakbah*. At the same time the unwholesome role of the Mufti of Jerusalem (who did collaborate with Hitler) is frequently trivialized. On the other hand, the same issue is still used by Israeli propaganda to discredit the Palestinian national movement altogether. Only recently has a balanced analysis emerged from Israeli and Palestinian scholars such as Zvi Elpeleg, Israel Gershoni, Philip Mattar, and Azmi Bishara.[9] Honest attempts to cope with this past still face an uphill struggle in the Arab and Muslim worlds. Just take the enthusiastic reception of Roger Garaudy and his Holocaust denial in Beirut, Cairo, and Damascus[10] in the late 1990s and the spread of anti-Semitic conspiracy theories after 9/11.[11]

All the more important are the voices of those Palestinian, Arab, and Muslim thinkers who challenge their societies on the issues of anti-Semitism and the Holocaust. Let's start with Azmi Bishara, who argued in a study published in 1994 that it is necessary for Arabs to deal with the Holocaust since Palestinians were directly or indirectly affected by this tragedy—and coexistence can only be reached by coping with the collective memories of both peoples. Arab anti-Jewish attitudes are not the *reason* but a *result* of the conflict.[12] But that does not make them less harmful. Hazem Saghiyeh deplores a mutual insistence on victimhood which does not contribute to understanding the sufferings of the other. The Holocaust has universal significance; dealing with it seriously does not constitute a "Zionist conspiracy" but a historical necessity.[13] And the late Edward Said asked how it was possible to demand the recognition of one's own trauma when refusing to recognize the trauma of the other, warning Arab intellectuals "who refuse to see the relationship between the Holocaust and Israel... I cannot accept the idea that the Holocaust excuses Zionism for what it has done to the Palestinians: far from it. I say exactly the opposite, that by recognizing the Holocaust for the genocidal madness it was, we can then demand from Israelis and Jews the right to link the Holocaust to Zionist injustices towards the Palestinians."[14]

Zionism and Anti-Semitism

So where does this all leave us with the fighters against the "New" and "Islamic" anti-Semitism?

First of all they underestimate the grave effects of a lasting conflict on the consciousness and sub-consciousness of the parties concerned. Had the Zionists decided—let's assume—to colonize Argentina, would an "Islamic anti-Semitism" flourish as well? Would Palestine have been colonized by—say—French Roman Catholics, could we not expect resistance to bear anti-Christian features? Would it not use memories of the Crusades?

Second, there is an underestimation of the effects of the U.S.-led war against international and Islamist terror. Can anybody talk about moods in the Arab-Islamic world without considering U.S. policies after 9/11 as well as the wars in Afghanistan and Iraq? Were not Jewish, pro-Israeli, pro-Likud politicians in the U.S. evidently involved in the elaboration of the "war on terror" against the "axis of evil"? Does any allusion to this state of affairs automatically constitute a reference to the "Protocols of the Elders of Zion"?[15]

Third, there is an underestimation of both the meaning of Israeli policies and the relationship between Israel and the official Jewish communities in the Diaspora. Does Sharon lead a colonial war against the Palestinians or not? Has he declared that he considers every Jew an "ambassador of Israel" or not?[16] Have official Jewish communities in Paris, London, and elsewhere not organized mass demonstrations under the slogan "solidarity with Israel" while Sharon's tanks and bulldozers devastated Jenin?[17] It is not only an "anti-Semitic" but also a Zionist paradox that links "every Jew, even if he does not want it with Israel—and Israel, even if it does not want, with every Jew."[18] Does not Brian Klug have a point in asking whether it is anti-Semitism pure and simple "when alienated Moroccan and Algerian youth in the [poor outskirts] of Paris, outraged by conditions in the occupied territories, attack Jewish individuals and institutions"? and then answering: "Fundamentally, it is an ethno-religious conflict between two communities with opposed identifications: roughly, French Muslims with Palestinian Arabs versus French Jews with Israeli Jews."[19] This is no consolation for the victims, but an adequate analysis is a precondition for adequate practical measures. "The semantic question has been politicized. This is why the definition matters. It is time to reclaim the word 'anti-Semitism' from the political misuses to which it is being put."[20]

And last not least, what would follow from a definition of the new forms of hostility as anti-Semitism? A war *à la* "war on terror"? After some reflection, would we have to realize that we are not dealing just with projections of a Hitlerite kind but have to face the maligned "root causes" after all? I am afraid much of the excitement about the "New anti-Semitism" is just meant to avoid these conclusions.

Notes

1. Antony Lerman, "Sense on Anti-Semitism," *Prospect Magazine* (August 2002).
2. Brian Klug, "The Collective Jew: Israel and the New Anti-Semitism," *Patterns of Prejudice* (June 2003): 1–19.
3. Dan Diner, "Ressentiment und Realität, Über Israel, Palästina und die Frage nach einem neuen Antisemitismus," manuscript, 2004; reprinted in Doron Rabinivici, Ulrich Speck and Natan Sznaider, eds., *Neuer Antisemitismus? Eine globale Debatte* (Frankfurt am Main: Suhrkamp, 2004).
4. Werner Bergmann, "Zur Entstehung von Feindbildern im Konflikt um Palästina," *Jahrbuch für Antisemitismus-Forschung*, 2003, pp. 15–21.
5. John Bunzl, *Juden im Orient* (Vienna: Junius, 1989); and John Bunzl, ed., *Islam, Judaism, and the Political Role of Religions in the Middle East* (Gainesville, Fl.: University Press of Florida, 2004).
6. Esther Webman, "Anti-Semitic Motifs in the Ideology of Hizbullah and Hamas," paper, Tel Aviv, 1989.
7. International Crisis Group (ICG), *Dealing with Hamas*, Amman/Brussels, September 3, 2004.
8. Yigal Carmon, "Harbingers of Change in the Anti-Semitic Discourse in the Arab World," MEMRI, April 23, 2003; Rainer Zimmer-Winkel and Götz Nordbruch, eds., *Die Araber und die Shoah* (Trier, 2000).
9. Zvi Elpeleg, *The Grand Mufti. Hadj Amin al-Hussaini* (London: Frank Cass, 1993); Israel Gershoni, *Rays of Light Piercing the Darkness: Egyptians Facing Fascism and Nazism* (Hebrew) (Tel Aviv, 1999); Philip Mattar, *The Mufti of Jerusalem* (rev. ed. New York: Columbia University Press, 1992); Azmi Bishara, "Die Araber und der Holocaust," in Rolf Steininger, ed., *Der Umgang mit dem Holocaust—Europa, U.S.A., Israel* (Vienna: Böhlau, 1994).
10. Götz Nordbruch, *Arab Reactions to Roger Garaudy's* The Founding Myths of Israeli Politics (Jerusalem, 2000).
11. Anti-Defamation League, "Spreading Anti-Semitism: Arab Media Blame Jews/Israel for Pushing U.S. to Brink of War," http://www.adl.org/Anti_semitism/arab/spreading_anti_semitism.asp, April 22, 2003.
12. Azmi Bishara, "Die Araber und der Holocaust," in Rolf Steininger, ed., *Der Umgang mit dem Holocaust.*
13. Hazem Saghiyeh, "Universalizing the Holocaust," *Palestine-Israel Journal* 3–4 (1998–99).
14. Edward Said, "A Reply to Arab Intellectuals," *Le Monde Diplomatique,* September 1998.
15. Michael Lind, "A Tragedy of Errors," *The Nation*, February 23, 2004.
16. Associated Press, February 21, 2003.
17. Jewish Agency, Press Release, April 8, 2002; Chris Gray, *The Independent,*

May 7, 2002.
18. Avirama Golan, "The Israel Connection," *Haaretz*, April 12, 2004.
19. Brian Klug, in exchange between Gidon D. Rema and Brian Klug, "Anti-Semitism: New or Old?" *The Nation*, April 12, 2004.
20. Ibid.

CHAPTER SEVEN

CAN THE EXPERIENCE OF DIASPORA JUDAISM SERVE AS A MODEL FOR ISLAM IN TODAY'S MULTICULTURAL EUROPE?

Sander L. Gilman

Two moments in modern history: a religious community in France is banned from wearing distinctive clothing in public schools as it is seen as an egregious violation of secular society; a religious community in Switzerland is forbidden from ritually slaughtering animals as such slaughter is seen as a cruel and unnatural act. These acts take place more than a hundred years apart: the former recently in France, the latter more than a century ago in Switzerland (where the prohibition against ritual slaughter still stands). But who are these religious communities? In France (among others) the order banning ostentatious religious clothing and ornaments in schools and other public institutions impacts as much on religious Jewish men who cover their heads (and perhaps even religious Jewish married women who cover their hair) as it does the evident target group, Muslim women. (The law is written in such a p.c. way as also to ban the ostentatious wearing of a cross: "Pierre, you can't come into school carrying that six-foot-high cross on your back. You will have to simply leave it in the hall.")

In Switzerland, even today the prohibition against kosher Jewish slaughter also covers the slaughter of meat by Moslems who follow the ritual practice ("dabh") that results in Halal meat. The Jewish practice was banned by the Nazis with the "Gesetz über das Schlachten von Tieren" ("Law on the Slaughtering of Animals") of 21 April 1933; it was sporadically permitted after 1945 through exceptions; only in 1997 were these exceptions made part of the legal code. The Islamic practice was outlawed in Germany until 1979 and even today is tolerated but not sanctioned.[1] These prohibitions impact on Jews and Muslims in oddly similar ways when Western responses to "slaughter" are measured. Very different is how the meat is used: whether in "traditional" dishes or in a "Big Mac." Indeed recently in France Odile Bonnivard offered an "identity" soup to coalesce French nativist sentiment. Shouting "we are all pig eaters!" her group (supported by the National Front) distribute "pig soup" to the poor on the streets of Paris, Strasbourg, and Nice. Halal and kosher foods are denounced as defining the difference of the Jews and Muslims from "European civilization and Christian culture." "Slices of oily sausages [were handed out] as flags bearing the French fleur-de-lis fluttered overhead."[2] The question is how did and will these two groups respond to such confrontation with the secular, "modern" world.[3]

Why should the focus of concern in secular Europe from the Enlightenment to today be on the practices and beliefs of Jews and on the Muslims? When the Sikhs in France raised the question of whether their turbans were "cultural" or "religious" symbols under the terms of the new regulations the official French spokesperson asked in effect: Are there Sikhs in France? Indeed there are.

Yet in September 2004, two French journalists were seized in Iraq and threatened with death unless the law limiting headscarves was not instituted the following week when school was to begin in France. The reaction was not a sense of support for the struggle for an Islamic identity in France. Indeed, virtually all of the French Muslim institutions, from the official French Council of the Muslim Faith to the radical Union of Islamic Organizations in France (UOIF), spoke out against the outside pressure even though it came from the "Islamic" world. As Olivier Roy, a leading French scholar of Islam, noted: "They may disagree on the law of the veil, but they are saying, 'This is our fight and don't interfere.' This is a pivotal moment."[4] Lhaj Thami Breze, the head of UOIF, who had been opposed to the law, proposed a compromise in which a moderate interpretation of the law would permit "modest head covering."[5] The unity of the Islamic community in France in opposition to the "law of the veil" was a sign of the development of a secular consciousness in this religious community. What was striking was that the majority of Muslim schoolgirls did not wear or quickly removed their head coverings the day school began. Only about 200 to 250 girls, mainly in Alsace, wore their scarves to school and all but about 100 removed them before entering the buildings. These were removed from the classroom and provided with "counseling" in the schools. For them the *hijab*, which had been seen as "a way to reconcile modernity, self-affirmation and authenticity," became was a sign of the Western rights they demanded as Muslims.[6] These were less central than the rule of law. Three male Sikh students in Bobigny, as Paris suburb, were sent home the first day of class for wearing their traditional head covering. This was true whether they saw the headscarf as a political or an ethnic or religious symbol. The demand that one see oneself as a citizen with the rights of the citizen to contest the claims of the secular state overrode any sense of the primary identification as a member of the *Ummah*, the Islamic religious community. Jacqueline Costa-Lascoux, research director at CEVIPOF, the Political Science Center of CRNR in Paris, noted that "the hostage taking has helped the Muslim community in France, mainly the young people, to understand that they can live in a democratic society and still be Muslims."[7] The operative terms here are "democratic society" and "Muslim." It is the constitution of the modern secular state and the need for religions such as Islam and Judaism to adapt to it that is at the heart of the matter.

Yet what does it mean to be a Muslim in this secular world of modern France? Scratch secular Europe today and you find all of the presuppositions and attitudes of Christianity concerning Jews and Muslims present in subliminal or overt forms. Secular society in Europe has absorbed Christianity into its very definition of the secular.[8] Indeed one can make an argument that "secular" society as we now see it in Europe is the result of the adaptation of Christianity to the model of secularism that arose as a compromise formation out of the wars of religion following the Reformation. The integration of the Jews into Enlightenment Europe, as Adam Sutcliffe has shown in his *Judaism and Enlightenment*, was integration into Christian Europe (with Christianity having different textures in England than in Holland than in Bavaria, etc.).[9] Whether one thinks this provided an ideal model for all modern states, as does the philosopher Charles Taylor when he claims secularization provides "people of different faiths, or different fundamental commitments" the ability to co-exist (33, 34) or whether one is leery of such claims as is Talal Asad, who sees this merely as a "political strategy" (3) the "Jewish template" may well provide a clue to the potentials for the processes that religious communities with specific ritual beliefs and practices confront.[10]

The veneer was that of a secular state, a veneer that did alter the nature of Christianity itself. Even if today it is true, as Richard Bulliet claims, that "Christianity and Judaism pass by definition the civilizational litmus tests proposed for Islam even though some of their [Jewish and Christian] practitioners dictate women's dress codes, prohibit alcoholic beverages, demand prayer in public schools, persecute gays and lesbians, and damn members of other faiths to hell,"[11] this was certainly not the case for Jews in the secularizing Christian world of the European nations and their colonies following the Reformation. Indeed, Jews were regularly seen as being inherently unable to pass "civilizational litmus tests" in the Western Diaspora in virtually all areas.

Yet even today there are odd and arcane echoes of older views about the meaning of Jewish ritual. In the mid-1990s there was a general acknowledgement in the Church that the *Bible for Christian Communities* (*La Bible Latino-américaine*), written by Bernard Hurault, a Catholic missionary based in Chile, to combat the raising tide of Evangelical

Christianity, was blatantly anti-Jewish. Eighteen million copies in English and Spanish were distributed in South America and hundreds of thousands sold in France and Belgium after it was published in May 1994. According to the text, the Jewish people killed Jesus Christ because they "were not able to control their fanaticism" and thus showed a true lack of decorum. It was also clear that Judaism was represented as a religion of meaningless rituals, mere "folkloric duties involving circumcision and hats."[12] (After a legal challenge from the French Jewish community, the text was officially withdrawn; it still circulates in South America.)

How such views are contested, sometimes successfully, sometimes unsuccessfully, is central to this tale; it also provides an interpretive framework through which to understand the debates about the meaning and function of Islam in the West that have taken place since 9/11. We need to recount the complex rethinking of what it meant and means to be Jewish in what in all intents and purposes remains a society rooted in specific images about Jewish adaptability and change.

Little has altered concerning the deep cultural legacy of Europe over the past two hundred years. Recently German, Italian, Polish, and Slovakian delegates demanded that the "Christian heritage" of the new Europe be writ large in the (failed) European constitution of 2005. It was only the post–September 11 anxiety of most states that enabled Valéry Giscard d'Estaing, as president of the convention writing the constitution, to persuade the group that such a reference would be "inappropriate." The demand was transformed into a reference in the preamble to the "cultural, religious, and humanist inheritance of Europe." No one missed what was meant. Certainly one of the things the French and Dutch referenda about the constitution in 2005 tested was the likelihood of admitting Turkey, a majority Muslim state, into the European Union. Judaism and Islam have an all-too-close relationship to Christianity and raise questions that remain troubling in Europe.

It is important not to reduce the relationship between Judaism and Islam to the role that Jewish ideas, concepts, and practices did or did not have in shaping the earliest forms of Islamic belief. It is clear that nineteenth-century Jewish scholars in Europe had a central role in examining the "Jewish roots" of historical Islam. Scholars from Abraham Geiger in the 1830s to Ignaz Goldziher at the end of the century stressed the Judaizing nature of early Islam. These roots, true or not, are not sufficient to explain the intense focus on the nature of Islam in Europe today. Islam is not simply a surrogate for speaking about the Jews in today's Europe because of superficial similarities to Judaism. Among Jewish scholars in the nineteenth century the search for the Jewish roots of Islam was certainly more than a surrogate for speaking about the relationship between Judaism and Christianity in the nineteenth century, as Susannah Heschel so elegantly shows in her study of *Abraham Geiger and the Jewish Jesus*.[13] At one moment, the examination or construction of Islam provided one major Jewish scholar with a model for the potential reform of contemporary Judaism. One can quote Goldziher's diaries: "I truly entered into the spirit of Islam to such an extent that ultimately I became inwardly convinced that I myself was a Muslim, and judiciously discovered that this was the only religion which, even in its doctrinal and official formulation, can satisfy philosophic minds. My ideal was to elevate Judaism to a similar rational level. Islam, so taught me my experience, is the only religion, in which superstitious and heathen ingredients are not frowned upon by the rationalism, but by the orthodox teachings."[14] For him the Islam he discovered becomes the model for a new spirit of Judaism at the close of the nineteenth century.

It is the seeming closeness of these "Abrahamic" religions and their joint history that draws attention to the real or imagined differences to the majority religion and its new form: secular society. The 'Abrahamic' religions" is the newest p.c. phrase: the "Judeo-Christian tradition" was the catch word for common aspects shared between Judaism and Christianity after the Holocaust made this an acceptable notion; "the Abrahamic religions" is the new buzzword including Islam into the Judeo-Christian fold that has become current only after 9/11. Both phrases attempt to defuse the clearly Christian aspects of modern Western secular society by expanding it, but, of course, only reemphasize it. Here Jonathan Sacks's notion of difference is helpful: in creating categories that elide difference, that stress superficial similarities, one believes that one is bridging "differences."[15] Actually one is submerging them.

The closeness of Christianity to Judaism and Islam results in what

Sigmund Freud called the "narcissism of minor differences." Those differences are heightened in this secular society, which is rooted in the mindset and often the attitudes, beliefs, social mores, and civic practices of the religious community—in Western Europe, Christianity. Thus in Western Europe there is a radical secularization of religious institutions in the course of the nineteenth century. Marriage is shifted from being solely in the control of the Church to being in the domain of the State: but this form of secularization still maintains the quasi-religious aura about marriage, something we see in the debates in France about gay marriage. No secularizing European state simply abandons marriage as a religious institution that has outlived its time, as nineteenth-century anarchists and some early twentieth-century radical Zionists claimed.[16] The new minority is promised a wide range of civil rights—including those of freedom of religion—if only they adhere to the standards of civilized behavior as defined by the secular society. This is rooted in the desire to make sure that that society with its masked religious assumptions redefines the minority's religious practice or "secularizes" a religious minority into an "ethnic" one.

Equally, it is vital not to confuse the experiences of contemporary Islam with the rhetoric of victimization often heard within Muslim communities in countries such as Germany. There the evocation of the Holocaust becomes a means of identifying with the iconic victims of German history, the Jews. Y. Michal Bodemann and Gökce Yurdakul have noted quite correctly how the competition for the space of the victim or of the essential Other has allowed Turkish writers, such as Yadé Kara, to call upon the Jews as the model, for good or for ill, for Turkish acculturation.[17] The Turkish community regularly evokes the Holocaust when it imagines itself. Thus at the public events in Berlin on 23 November 2002 commemorating the horrendous murder of Turkish immigrants in Mölln in 1992, one heard the Turkish spokesman, Safter Çınar, evoke the experience of the Jews in the Holocaust as the model by which the contemporary experience of Turks could be measured. The power of this analogy is clear. But this self-conscious evocation of the experience of the Jews is only one aspect of contemporary parallels of Jews and Muslims.

Let us now look at the experiences within the various strands of

Jewish religious (and therefore social) ritual practice from the late eighteenth century (which marked the beginning of civil emancipation) that parallel those now confronting Diaspora Islam in "secular" Western Europe.[18] The similarities are striking: a religious minority enters into a self-described secular (or secularizing) society which is Christian in its rhetoric and presuppositions and which perceives a "special relationship" with this minority. The co-territorial society sees this as an act of aggression. This minority speaks a different secular language but also has yet a different religious language. This is odd in countries that have a national language and (in some) a religious language but not a secular language spoken by a religious minority as well as a ritual. Religious schools that teach in the languages associated with a religious group are seen as sources of corruption and illness. Religious rites are practiced that seem an abomination to the majority "host" culture: unlike the secular majority these religious communities practice the mutilation of children's bodies (infant male circumcision, and, for some Muslims, infant female genital cutting); the suppression of the rights of women (lack of women's traditional education; a secondary role in religious practice; arranged marriages; honor killings); barbaric torture of animals (the cutting of the throats of unstunned animals allowing them to bleed to death); disrespect for the dead through too rapid burial; ritual excess (in the case of the Jews, drunkenness at Purim; feasting during Ramadan in the case of the Muslims); ostentatious clothing that signals religious affiliation and has ritual significance (from women's hair covering such as the Muslim hijab to Jewish sheitels to men's hats such as the Jewish stremil or the Muslim taqiyah). Centrally relating all of these practices is a belief in the divine "chosenness" of the group in contrast to all others. The demonization of aspects of religious practice has its roots in what civil society will tolerate and what it will not; what it considers to be decorous and what is unacceptable as a social practice. Why it will not tolerate something is, of course, central to the story. Thus Alan Dundes argued a decade ago that the anxiety about meanings associated with the consumption of the body and blood of Christ in the Christian Mass shaped the fantasy of the Jews as slaughtering Christian children for their blood.[19] But it is equally present in the anger in secular Europe directed at Jewish ritual practices such as ritual slaughter with its obligatory bloodletting.

One of the most striking similarities of the process of integration into Western secular society is the gradual elision of the striking national differences among the various groups. Muslims in Western Europe represent multiple national traditions (South Asian in the U.K., North African in France and Spain, Turkish in Germany). But so did the Jews in Western Europe who came out of ghettos in France and the Rhineland, from the rural reaches of Bavaria and Hungary, who moved from those parts of "Eastern Europe"—Poland, the eastern Marches of the Austro-Hungarian Empire—which became part of the West and from the fringes of Empire to the centre. To this one can add the Sephardi Jews from the Iberian Peninsula who settled in areas from Britain (introducing fish and chips) to the fringes of the Austrian Empire. The standard image of the Jews in eighteenth-century British caricature was the Maltese Jew in his oriental turban. By the nineteenth century it was that of Lord Rothschild in formal wear receiving the Prince of Wales at his daughter's wedding in a London synagogue. Religious identity (as the Jew or the Muslim) replaced national identity—by then few (except the anti-Semites) remembered that the Rothschilds were a Frankfurt family that escaped the Yiddish-speaking ghetto. The "Jews" are everywhere and all alike; Muslims seem to be everywhere and are becoming "all alike." Even ritual differences and theological antagonism seem to be diminished in the Diaspora where the notion of a Muslim *Ummah* (or community) seems to be realized. It is the ideal state, to quote Talal Asad, of "being able to live as autonomous individuals in a collective life that exists beyond national borders."[20] But this too has its pitfalls, as the "Jewish template" shows.

Now for Jews in those lands that would become Germany, in the Austro-Hungarian Empire, in France, and in those lands that would become Great Britain, the stories are all different: different forms of Christianity, different expectations as to the meaning of citizenship. Different notions of secularization all present slightly different variations on the theme of what you have to give up to become a true citizen. Do you merely have to give up your secular language (Western and Eastern Yiddish, Ladino, Turkish, Urdu, colloquial Arabic)? Today there has been a strong suggestion in Germany and the United Kingdom that preaching in the mosques be done only in English—for security reasons. Do you have to abandon the most evident and egregious practices, or must you, as the German philosopher Johann Gottlieb Fichte (1762–1814) states (echoing debates about Jewish emancipation during the French revolution), "cut off their Jewish heads and replace them with German ones"?[21] And that was not meant as a metaphor, but as a statement of the impossibility of Jewish transformation into Germans.

What aspects of being "Jewish" in terms of Jewish religious practice and belief did Jews think it possible to change in the eighteenth and nineteenth century? What did the acceptance or rejection of such practices or beliefs accomplish or not accomplish within various national states? That is, what was gained and what was lost? We have to imagine this both in terms of the ability of all living religions to transform themselves and the clear understanding that all such transformations generate resistance and thus call forth other forms of religious practice in response. All of these changes deal in general with question of Jewish "identity" but in a complex and often contradictory manner. For the history of the Jews in the European Diaspora the late eighteenth century called forth three great "reformers" who took on different reforms in the light of the Diaspora status of the Jews: Moses Mendelssohn (1729–1786) and the followers of the Jewish Enlightenment in Germany (and their predecessors in Holland) who confronted a secularizing world. Rabbi Eliyahu of Vilnius—the Vilna Gaon (1720–1797)—in the Baltic, who desired to reform tradition Orthodoxy to make it more able to function in a self-contained Jewish world. The first modern Jewish mystics, the Hasidim, typified by Rabbi Yisrael, the Baal Shem Tov (the Master of the Good Name) (1698–1760), who fought, like their contemporaries in Berlin and Vilnius against what they saw as the stultifying practices and worldview of contemporary Judaism. All lived roughly simultaneously. In their wake came radical changes in what it meant to be a Jew in belief and practice. For contemporary Islam, all can serve as answers to the pressures found throughout the Diaspora. All offer parallels to the dilemmas faced by Islam in the West today. Thus the list of "abominations" that secular Europe saw in Jewish ritual practices became the earmark for the question of what Jews were willing to change in order to better fit the various national assumptions about citizenship. These were as different in the nineteenth century as the debates about Islamic head covering in the twenty-first century in France—opposed because it violates the idea of a secular state; Germany—supportive under the very different meanings of multiculturalism; and the United Kingdom, where in March 2005 the courts allowed full traditional South Asian clothing (the *jilbab*) as an exception to the "school uniform" rule in a predominantly Muslim school where the dress code had been worked out with the parents.[22]

Now I know that there are also vast differences between Jews in the eighteenth and nineteenth centuries and Muslims today. There are simply many more Muslims today in Western Europe than there were Jews in the earlier period. The Jews historically never formed more than 1 percent of the population of any Western European nation. Muslim populations form a considerable minority today. While there is no Western European city with a Muslim majority, many recent news stories predict that Marseilles or Rotterdam will be the first European city which will have one. In France today there are 600,000 Jews, while there are between 5 and 6 million Muslims, who make up about 10 percent of the population. In Germany, with a tiny Jewish population of slightly over 100,000, almost 4 percent of the population is Muslim (totaling more than 3 million people). In Britain about 2.5% percent of the total population (1.48 million people) is Muslim.[23] Demographics (and birthrate) aside, there are salient difference in the experiences of the Jews and Muslims in the past and today. The Jews had no national "homeland"—indeed were defined as nomads or a pariah people (pace Max Weber and Hannah Arendt). They lived only in the *Goles*, the Diaspora, and seemed thus inherently different from any other people in Western Europe (except perhaps the Roma). Most Muslims in the West come out of a national tradition often formed by colonialism in which their homelands had long histories disturbed but not destroyed by colonial rule. And, last but not least, the Israel-Palestinian conflict over the past century (well before the creation of the state of Israel), the establishment of a Jewish homeland as well as the Holocaust seems to place the two groups—at least in the consciousness of the West—into two antagonistic camps.[24]

Religion for the Jews of pre-Enlightenment Europe and for much of contemporary Islam, which has its immediate roots in majority Islamic states, became for many a "heritage" in the Western, secular Diaspora. What had been lived experiences in *milieux de memoire* (environment of memory), to use Pierre Nora's often-cited phrase from 1994, become *lieux de memoire*—places of memory—that refigure meaning constantly within the Diaspora.[25] What is it that such memory of ritual and practice can or must abandon? What must it preserve to maintain its coherence for the group? The answer depends on time and place, and yet the experience of Jews in the Western European Diaspora seems to offer a model case clearly because of the "narcissism of minor differences" among the three Abrahamic religions. The Jews maintain, in different modalities, their religious identity, even if the nature of the options explored created ruptures that produced their new problems and over time partial resolutions and yet further conflicts and resolutions. Thus the ultra-conservative Sephardi Rabbi Ovadiah Yosef, former Chief Sephardi Rabbi of Israel, today applauds the use of aesthetic surgery to improve the marriageable status of women and men.[26]

The central cultural issue of the New Europe is not European integration in national terms, but the relationship between secular society and the dynamic world of European Islam. As the Syrian-born German sociologist Bassam Tibi noted decades ago, it is the struggle within Islam to become a modern religion, whether within Islamic world or in the Islamic Diaspora in the West, that is central.[27] Recently further voices, such as those of Tariq Ramadan and Feisal Abdul Rauf, have noted the need for a "modern" Islam.[28] There are certainly moments of confrontation in which Islamic ritual and practices have changed in specific settings. One can think of the entire history of Bosnian Islam from the nineteenth century until its destruction in the past decade and the resultant fundamentalist cast given Bosnia over the past decade. There is, however, a substantial difference between the contexts. Any one interested in contemporary Europe before 9/11/2001 knew that the eight-hundred-pound gorilla confronting France, Germany, and the United Kingdom—and to a lesser extent Spain and Italy—was the huge presence of an "unassimilatable" minority. Given Samuel Huntington's recent pronouncements about Hispanics in the United States—"The persistent inflow of Hispanic immigrants threatens to divide the United

States into two peoples, two cultures, and two languages. Unlike past immigrant groups, Mexicans and other Latinos have not assimilated into mainstream U.S. culture, forming instead their own political and linguistic enclaves—from Los Angeles to Miami—and rejecting the Anglo-Protestant values that built the American dream. The United States ignores this challenge at its peril"[29]—the question of Muslims in Western Europe seemed to forecast the same set of problems. But, of course, exactly the same things were said (with correction for national self-image) about the Jews for two hundred years.

Notes

1. Rupert Jentzsch, "Das rituelle Schlachten von Haustieren in Deutschland ab 1933" (Diss., Hannover, Tierärztliches Hochschul, 1998).
2. Craig S. Smith, "Poor and Muslim? Jewish? Soup Kitchen is Not for You," *The New York Times* (28 February 2006): A4.
3. For deep background see Jonathan M. Hess, *Germans, Jews, and the Claims of Modernity* (New Haven: Yale University Press, 2002).
4. Elaine Sciolino, "Ban on Head Scarves Takes Effect in a United France," *The New York Times* (September 3, 2004): A9.
5. "A Tragic Twist of the Scarf," *The Economist* (September 4, 2004): 49.
6. Olivier Roy, *Globalised Islam: The Search for the New Ummah* (London: Hurst & Co., 2004), p. 24.
7. Tom Hundley, "'No Strikes, no Sit-ins' over France's Scarf Ban," *The Chicago Tribune* (September 8, 2004): 6.
8. Here I reflect the debates about "secularization" that have dominated much of the past half-century from Carl Becker to Hannah Arendt to M. H. Abrams to Peter Berger to Hans Blumenberg's *The Legitimacy of the Modern Age* and beyond. Elizabeth Brient, "Hans Blumenberg and Hannah Arendt on the 'Unworldly Worldliness' of the Modern Age," *Journal of the History of Ideas* 61 (2000): 513–30.
9. Adam Sutcliffe, *Judaism and Enlightenment* (Cambridge: Cambridge University Press, 2003).
10. See Charles Taylor, "Models of Secularism," in Rajeev Bhargava, ed., *Secularism and Its Critics* (Delhi: Oxford University Press, 1998), pp. 31–53, and Talal Asad, *Formations of the Secular: Christianity, Islam, Modernity* (Stanford: Stanford University Press, 2003).
11. Richard W. Bulliet, *The Case for Islamo-Christian Civilization* (New York: Columbia University Press, 2004), p. 12.
12. "French Bishop Orders Recall of Anti-Semitic Bible," *The Associated Press*

(March 9, 1995, Thursday, AM cycle).

13. Susannah Heschel, *Abraham Geiger and the Jewish Jesus* (Chicago: University of Chicago Press,1998).

14. Ignaz Goldziher, *Tagebuch*, ed. Alexander Scheiber (Leiden: Brill, 1978), p. 59.

15. Jonathan Sacks, *The Dignity of Difference: How to Avoid the Clash of Civilizations* (London: Continuum, 2002). See also Richard Harries, "[On] Jonathan Sacks, *The Dignity of Difference; How to Avoid the Clash of Civilisations* (2002)," *Scottish Journal of Theology* 57 (2004): 109–15.

16. David Biale, *Eros and the Jews* (Berkeley: University of California Press, 1997).

17. Y. Michal Bodemann, Gökce Yurdaku, "Diaspora lernen: Wie sich türkische Einwanderer an den Juden in Deutschland orientieren," *Süddeutsche Zeitung* (2 November 2005) and "Geborgte Narrative: Wie sich türkische Einwanderer an den Juden in Deutschland orientieren," *Soziale Welt* 56 (2005): 11–33.

18. For an excellent case study of the adaptation of Judaism as religious practice in the American Diaspora see Jenna Joselit, *The Wonders of America: Reinventing American Jewish Culture 1880–1950* (New York: Hill and Wang, 1994).

19. Alan Dundes, *The Blood Libel Legend* (Madison: The University of Wisconsin Press, 1991).

20. Asad, op. cit., p. 180.

21. See Michael Mack, *German Idealism and the Jew* (Chicago: University of Chicago Press, 2003).

22. The complexity of this position is highlighted in the essays collected by Janet R. Jakobsen and Ann Pellegrini, eds., "World Secularisms at the Millennium," *Social Text* 18.3 (2000). See specifically their introduction on pp. 1–27.

23. See the essay by Ranu Samantrai, "Continuity or Rupture? An Argument for Secular Britain," *Social Text* 18.3 (2000): 105–21.

24. Two polemical but informative books shape their argument about contemporary Islamic identity primarily around the rhetoric of the Israeli-Palestinian conflict rather than this being seen as part of the struggle about the modernization of Islam both within and beyond Europe: Jack Goody, *Islam in Europe* (London: Polity, 2004), and Gilles Kepel, *The War for Muslim Minds: Islam and the West*, trans. Pascale Ghazaleh (Cambridge: Belknap Press / Harvard University Press, 2004). See also Ella Shohat, "Columbus, Palestine and Arab-Jews: Toward a Relational Approach to Community Identity," in Keith Ansell-Pearson, Benita Parry, and Judith Squires, eds., *Cultural Readings of Imperialism: Edward Said and the Gravity of History* (New York: St. Martin's, 1997), pp. 88–105, and Asad, op. cit, pp. 158–80.

25. Pierre Nora, ed., *Les Lieux de mémoire*, vol. 1: *Les France: Conflits et partages* (Paris: Gallimard, 1993).

26. Zion Zohar, "Oriental Jewry Confronts Modernity: The Case of Rabbi Ovadiah Yosef," *Modern Judaism* 24 (2004): 120–49, here, 132–33.

27. See Bassam Tibi, *Krieg der Zivilisationen* (Hamburg: Hoffmann & Campe, 1995). His work is available in English *The Challenge of Fundamentalism* (University of California Press, 2002) and *Islam Between Culture and Politics* (New York: Palgrave Macmillan, 2002).

28. Tariq Ramadan, *Western Muslims and the Future of Islam* (New York: Oxford University Press, 2003); Feisal Abdul Rauf, *What's Right with Islam: A New Vision for Muslims and the West* (San Francisco: HarperSanFrancisco, 2004).

29. Samuel P. Huntington, "The Hispanic Challenge," *Foreign Policy* (March/April 2004), pp. 1–16; later included in his *Who Are We: The Challenges to America's National Identity* (New York: Simon & Schuster, 2004).

CHAPTER EIGHT

BRIDGING THE UNBRIDGEABLE:
The Holocaust and Al-Nakba

Dan Bar-On and Saliba Sarsar

Palestinians and Israeli Jews are deeply committed to the same tiny piece of land, from which both generate their identities and histories. The conflict has resulted in a total separation between them, and this is expressed through their respective narratives, rituals, and myths, which compress the present into the past and mobilize the future. If the 1993 Oslo Accords created the hope that the two peoples were moving out of a hundred years of conflict, the current cycle of violence that began in September 2000 has created new depths of despair and frustration. The deeper both peoples descend into the abyss of dehumanization and victimization, the farther they move from the possibility of mutual acceptance, healing, and hope.

Each side tries to justify its own moral superiority. Palestinians usually start from the Balfour Declaration in 1917, move through the British Mandate, the first Arab-Israeli War of 1948 and the Israeli occupation of Palestinian lands since 1967 (Farsoun and Zacharia, 1997). These events appear as one continuous tragedy in Palestinian minds, and are often blamed on Zionism and its exclusionary ideology (Said, 1980; Masalha, 1992). Palestinians living in Israel, in the West Bank and Gaza Strip, or in exile, experience Palestine as real and its Jewish usurpers as victimizers. Rashid Khalidi writes,

"...Israelis, many of them descended from victims of persecution, pogroms, and concentration camps, have themselves been mistreating another people" (1997:5). There is still a deep-felt wish among many Palestinians that the Jewish State will just "evaporate."

Jews view the return to their ancestral homeland after two thousand years of exile as a miracle. Many consider it a return of "people without land to a land without people." They see the Palestinians as an unexpected and unwelcome interference. They would like to wake up one day, to find the land empty and their memories freed from this "bad dream."

How can one move out of this mutual exclusivity and into mutual acceptance of the other after so many years of hatred and loss?

The Catch of Victimhood

We can forgive people in our heads without forgiving them in our hearts.

For the former to become the latter, it must be, in Freud's phrase, "worked through." Psyche and soma, which have been divided by trauma, must be reunited again. This means shifting the past out of the present; replacing psychological simultaneity with linear sequence; slowly loosening the hold of a grief and an anger whose power traps us in an unending yesterday. (Ignatieff, 1998: 164–5).

Michael Ignatieff made these insights while citing Stephen Daedalus of Joyce's *Ulysses*: "History is a nightmare from which I am trying to awake." He reached the conclusion by looking at several current ethnic conflicts, in which peacemaking (that is represented usually by the "heads") and peace building (that is ordinarily dependent on the "guts") are still far apart. What mechanisms separate "head" and "heart" or "psyche" and "soma," even when top-down peacemaking is under way?

The feeling of "being victims" is normally based on solid individual and collective experiences during protracted violent conflict. These experiences gain a powerful grip on identity construction, however, when they are transformed in the collective memory into myths and transmitted from one generation to the next through memoirs and family stories, school books (Bar-Tal, 1997), and national symbolic acts and festivals (Ross, 1999). Today, many Palestinians are probing the past and present, both to reconstruct and remember history and to transmit its lessons to future generations. (Said, 1999; Barghouti, 2003; Shehadeh, 2003).

When one asks Palestinians where they come from, they will promptly name a village or town they themselves might have never inhabited, but their grandparents had left, or were forced to leave. Some will even show rusted keys and torn documents inherited from parents and grandparents as proof of land or house ownership. The Israeli Jewish context is still dominated by the myths of "fertilizing the empty land" and "the few against the many" relating to the 1948 war, preventing them from reaching beyond their own ethnocentric thinking and feeling the plight of the "other."

Exclusion of the "Other"

Both sides identify themselves as victimized by the other. Rarely, though, are such long-term conflicts symmetrical. Usually, one can define one party as the more powerful, trying to coerce, exclude, or de-legitimize the other. Conflicts can be divided according to their level of asymmetry. The most complex are those in which there is no agreement on the measures used to decide which is the more powerful party. Palestinians typically view Israeli Jews as being more powerful, militarily and economically. Israeli Jews feel threatened by the demographic immensity of the whole Arab-Muslim world, relating it to their previous experiences of being a minority in Europe and Afro-Asia for many generations. They cannot accept the Palestinian perspective of the current asymmetrical power division, as it does not relate to their own fears of being overwhelmed demographically.

In the Israeli-Palestinian context, the mutual feelings of victimization are best illustrated by two historical events that are the cornerstones for the collective memories of the Palestinians and the Israeli Jews. These are the Holocaust (*Shoah* in Hebrew) and the Catastrophe (*Al-Nakba* in Arabic); the exodus of Palestinians in 1948 and the resultant refugee problem. Generally, both sides mourn their own man-made cataclysms separately. There is an underlying fear that the acknowledgement of the tragedy of the "other" will justify their moral superiority and imply acceptance of their collective rationale. For the Palestinians, accepting the Jewish pain around the Holocaust means accepting the moral ground for the creation of the State of Israel. For the Israeli Jews, accepting the pain of the 1948 Palestinian refugees means sharing responsibility for their plight and their right of return.

The Yad Vashem Holocaust Memorial and the ruins of Deir Yassin lie close together, west of Jerusalem, but are a world apart in the psyche of Jews and Palestinians. While the former commemorates the systematic mass extermination of European Jews under the Nazi occupation prior to and during World War II, the latter is the village where 254 Palestinians were massacred at the hands of Jewish extremists in April 1948. It symbolizes Palestinian dispossession and the struggle for self-determination. Jews and Palestinians have been steadfast in their different interpretations of past events and current realities, refusing to participate in each other's painful memories, and thereby denying each other's past.

Following two visits to Yad Vashem, Ghassan Abdallah, a Palestinian activist, wrote: "We were never responsible for the pogroms and discrimination against Jews in Europe .... So why should Palestinians pay for the crimes of Europeans against Jews? What Palestinians and Arabs are up against is modem political Zionism, with its invasion of our historic land and culture, using false myths and pretenses." (2002: 43) This is a typical Palestinian reaction to the pain of the Jewish people, rejecting it as being invalid from their own perspective. Even while stating a truth (Palestinians were not responsible for the Jewish plight during the Holocaust), Abdallah missed the opportunity to empathize with the deep pain that Jews feel when they come to Yad Vashem. Conversely, when Yasser Arafat wanted to visit the Holocaust Museum in Washington, D.C., in 1998, American Jews turned him down, interpreting his wish as a manipulation of their most sacred feelings. The history of the two peoples is full of similar missed opportunities.

There are many instances in which Palestinians have questioned the validity of the Holocaust, expressing an underlying logic that "the enemies of our enemies are our friends." At the 1998 Hamburg meeting of the TRT (To Reflect and Trust) group,[1] FS (a Palestinian woman from Gaza) asked on the fourth day of the encounter, "How do you know there was a Holocaust?" The Jewish participants were shocked. They felt she was disqualifying the stories of their parents which they shared earlier. The crisis that arose required the intervention of a German participant who told FS about his father's involvement in the atrocities. Only then could she accept these facts. It became clear she had never learned about the Holocaust in school or college.

There are also many Israeli-Jewish examples of ethnocentricity (Steinberg & Bar-On, 2002). In a recent visit of Israeli (Jewish and Palestinian) and German students at Buchenwald concentration camp, Jewish students left the camp agitated. They let their feelings surface by expressing anger toward the Palestinian students rather than the Germans who participated in the tour. The Jewish participants perceived the Palestinians' behavior as "inappropriate." Some of the Jewish students felt that the Palestinians ignored Jewish suffering in the camp and thus did not meet Jewish expectations of the experience in this memorial context. Following the visit, the Palestinian leader wrote that he felt the Jewish students vented their anger on the Palestinian students, anger that had nothing to do with them. The Jews could not express their anger about the Holocaust directly toward the Germans. He felt this reflected a pattern of displaced Israeli aggression (Halaby, 1999). In another workshop at Ben Gurion University, the Jewish and the Palestinian groups convened separately on the day of Al-Nakba. The Palestinians approached the Jewish group to invite them to join their memorial ritual, and were deeply hurt when none of the Jewish participants came to stand with them for the minute of silence (Bar-On & Kassem, in press). This was later addressed and worked through in joint group sessions.

Beyond Victimhood: A New Beginning

Only recently have some Israeli Jewish and Palestinian intellectuals found the courage to bridge this gap. On the Israeli Jewish side, for example, Ilan Gur-Zeev and Ilan Pappe have called for the Holocaust and Al-Nakba to be examined within a mutual context (2003). Their argument does not claim equivalence between the two events but rather highlights the thread that ties them to the collective psyche of both people. Hence, they raise the serious need for each side to recognize the pain, morality, and legitimacy of the other's narrative, without raising any issue of moral superiority. Benny Morris's historical research (1999), while not always critical or objective (Finkelstein, 2001: 51–87), established a new Jewish understanding of the Israeli government and military command role in the expulsion of Palestinians during the 1948 war.

On the Palestinian side, Azmi Bishara (1996), Edward W. Said (1997), and Father Nairn S. Ateek (2001) connected Palestinian acknowledgement of the Holocaust to Israeli Jewish recognition of the Palestinian Catastrophe and dispossession. "In order for the victim to forgive," Bishara (1992:6) argued, "he must be recognized as a victim. That is the difference between a historic compromise and a cease-fire." In examining the foundations for peace, Ateek (2001: 168–69) urges Palestinians to develop a new attitude toward the Holocaust. He explains, "We must understand the importance and significance of the Holocaust to the Jews, while insisting that the Jews understand the importance and significance of the tragedy of Palestine for the Palestinians." Hazem Saghiyeh and Saleh Bashir go further by suggesting in *Al-Hayat* (2000) that "the Arabs will not gain anything by ignoring or denying the Holocaust. Continuing such denial, paradoxically, can even be facilitative for Israel."

Recently, Arab-Israeli pupils have joined Jewish schoolmates on trips to Poland. In this spirit, Father Emil Shoufani and his Jewish partner Ruth Bar-Shalev introduced the From Memory to Peace initiative, to "establish a better understanding for the pain the Jews suffered in Europe during World War II and how it affects them until this day" (Lavy, 2003). Ester Golan, a Jewish participant who lost her parents in the

Holocaust and journeyed with Father Shoufani and 250 others to Auschwitz-Birkenau, views the initiative as "a way of healing old wounds." In her journal, she writes: "Let us stay on the 'Connecting Path' and live for a better future for us all. As Father Shoufani repeatedly said: 'We have to grow from within.' We all grew. We all changed, each in his or her own way. That is what it is all about."[2] However, the Israeli Jewish public still has great difficulty finding ways to participate, even symbolically, in the Palestinian commemoration of AI-Nakba.

Our duty is to question past mistakes and end the cycle of violence by changing attitudes from "who desires peace, prepare for war" to "who desires peace, prepare for peace." Our mission is to acknowledge the pain and suffering of the "other" as part of the process of conciliation that will take place between the two peoples once the Palestinian state is established and mutual violent acts end. This is part of our moral obligation toward each other. Dialogue between Israeli Jews and Palestinians must include an inward look into one's own culture and society and an outward look into the "other's" culture and society (Sarsar, 2002b). If dialogue is to be a sustainable, ongoing process, each national community must acknowledge and respect the other's pain, whether it was party to its creation or not. Such an inclusive act of communication and faith will prepare the way for working through the past and building peace. Our future and the future of our children and grandchildren depend on it.

Notes

1. The TRT group was originally composed of descendants of Holocaust survivors and descendants of Nazi perpetrators (Bar-On, 1995). In 1998 practitioners from current conflicts (South Africa, Northern Ireland and Palestinians and Israelis) joined the group to test the possibility that the story telling method the group developed could also be used in these conflicts (Bar-On, 2000).
2. Excerpted from Golan's personal account of the journey, e-mailed to Saliba Sarsar in August 2003.

Bibliography

Abdallah, G. "A Palestinian at Yad Vashem," *Jerusalem Quarterly File* 15 (Winter 2002): 42–45.

Alcallay, A. *After Jews and Arabs*. University of Minnesota Press, 1993.

Ateek, N. S. *Justice and Only Justice: A Palestinian Theology of Liberation*. Maryknoll, N.Y.: Orbis Books, 1989 and 2001.

Barghouti, M. *I Saw Ramallah*. New York: Anchor Books, 2003.

Bar-On, D. "Encounters between Descendants of Nazi Perpetrators and Descendants of Holocaust Survivors." *Psychiatry* 58, no. 3 (1995): 225–45.

Bar-On, D. *Bridging the Gap*. Hamburg: Kerber-Stiftung, 2000.

Bar-On, D. *The "Other" Within Us: Changes in the Israeli Identity from a Psychosocial Perspective* (Hebrew). Jerusalem: Mossad Bialik & Ben Gurion University, 1999.

Bar-On, D., and Kassem, F. "Storytelling as a Way to Work-Through Intractable Conflicts: The TRT German-Jewish Experience and its Relevance to the Palestinian-Israeli Context." *Social Issues*. In press.

Bar-Tal, D. "Formation and Change of Ethnic and National Stereotypes: An Integrative Model." *International Journal of Intercultural Relations* 21, no. 4 (1997): 491–523.

Bishara, A. "On Chauvinism and Universalism" (in Hebrew). *Zemanim* 55 (Winter 1996): 102–107.

Bishara, A. "Between Place and Space" (in Hebrew). *Studio* 37 (October 1992).

Farsoun, S. K. with Zacharia, C. E. *Palestine and the Palestinians*. Boulder, Colo.: Westview Press, 1997.

Khalidi, R. *Palestinian Identity: The Construction of Modern National Consciousness*. New York: Columbia University Press, 1997.

Gur-Zeev, I., and I. Pappe, "Beyond the Destruction of the Other's Collective Memory: Blueprints for a Palestinian-Israeli Dialogue." *Theory, Culture*

& *Society* 20, no. 1 (February 2003): 93–108.

Halaby, R. "On the Visit of Israeli Jewish and Palestinian Students to Buchenwald" (in German). *Babylon* (1999): 67–78.

Ignatieff, M. *The Warrior's Honor.* New York: Henry Holt–Owl Books, 1998.

Lavy, A. "Arabs Travel to Auschwitz" (in Hebrew). *Haaretz* (February 7, 2003).

Masalha, N. *Expulsion of the Palestinians.* Washington, D.C.: Institute of Palestine Studies, 1992.

Morris, B. *Righteous Victims.* New York: Knopf, 1999.

Ross, M. H. *The Culture of Conflict: Interpretations and Interests in Comparative Perspective.* New Haven, Conn.: Yale University Press.

Rouhana, N. N., and D. Bar-Tal. "Psychological Dynamics of Intractable Ethnonational Conflicts: The Israeli-Palestinian Case." *American Psychologist* 53 (1998): 761–70.

Saghiyeh, H., and S. Bashir. "The Holocaust of the Jews, Al-Nakba of the Palestinians" (Translated from *Al-Hayat*). *Haaretz* (February 21, 2000).

Sagy, S., S. Steinberg, and M. Fahiraladin. "The Self in the Society and the Society in the Self: Two Ways to Look at a Group Process Between Jewish and Palestinian Students in Israel" (in German). *Babylon* 19 (1999): 48–66.

Said, E. W. *The Question of Palestine.* New York: Vintage, 1980.

Said, E. W. "Bases for Coexistence." *Al-Ahram Weekly* (November 15, 1997).

Said, E. W. *Out of Place: A Memoir.* New York: Alfred A. Knopf, 1999.

Sarsar. S. "Reconciling the Children of Abraham." *Peace Review* 14, no. 3 (2002a): 319–24.

Sarsar. S. "Jerusalem and Peacemaking in Arab Palestinian and Israeli Jewish Relations." *Clio's Psyche* 9.3 (December 2002b): 136–38.

Shehadeh, R. *Strangers in the House: Coming of Age in Occupied Palestine.* New York: Penguin Books, 2003.

Steinberg, S., and D. Bar-On. "An Analysis of the Group Process in Encounters between Jews and Palestinians Using a Typology for Discourse Classification." *International Journal of Intercultural Relations* 26 (2002): 199–214.

CHAPTER NINE

THE ANTI-SEMITISM
OF HAMAS

Meir Litvak

Anti-Semitism is a major pillar in the ideology of Hamas (acronym of *Harakat al-muqawama al-Islamiyya*—Islamic Resistance Movement), a Palestinian national-Islamic movement, which perceives and articulates its conflict with Israel in Manichean and absolutist religious terms. Like most other Islamic movements in the Middle East, Hamas regards the conflict as the latest and most fateful phase of the relentless onslaught waged by western imperialism and culture against Islam since the Crusades. Hamas publications portray the Jews as instruments of the West or, alternatively, as the power that controls and manipulates the West in this war. Concurrently, it views the current struggle as the last link in the war, which the Jews have been waging against Islam since its essence. Consequently, Hamas emphasizes the "Islamic essence" of the Palestinian cause.

As such, the struggle is portrayed as an unbridgeable dichotomy between two absolutes: a "war of religion and faith," between Islam and

Judaism and between Muslims and Jews, rather than one between Palestinians and Israelis or Zionists.

It is a historical, religious, cultural, and existential conflict between the true religion, which supersedes all previous religions, i.e. Islam, and the abrogated superseded religion, Judaism. It is a war between good personified by the Muslims who represent the party of God (*Hizballah*) against "evil incarnated…. the party of Satan" (*hizb al-shaytan*) represented by the Jews.[1]

Justifying the Self and Demonizing the Other

Every conflict involves justification of the Self and the demonization of rivals and enemies, or in Hamas' case the Jews as the "enemies of God and of humanity." Such an accusation, in the words of Bernard Lewis, applies to all enemies of Islam since, if according to the Quran the fighters for Islam are fighting in holy war "in the path of God" and for God, then their opponents are fighting against God and are, therefore, his enemies.[2] However, such depiction is used more forcefully and more often against the Jews in view of their explicit castigation by the Quran.

Unlike the non-Islamist Palestinian groups, Hamas makes no distinction between Judaism and Zionism, and uses "Zionists" and "Jews" synonymously and interchangeably. Judaism is a "religion that stipulates racism and hostility towards others in its books and incites to usurp unjustly Palestine under the slogan of the Holy Land." Zionism, according to this view, transforms these Jewish ideas into reality. Likewise, terrorism is an integral and inherent pillar of Judaism, which stems from the teaching of the Torah, and it finds its expression in Zionist massacres in Palestine.[3]

The portrayal of the Jews as powerful archenemies of Islam departs from traditional Islamic depictions of the Jews that are associated with cowardice, degradation, and wretchedness. It has become a central element in Hamas' ideology and an important theme in the writings of all Islamist movements in the Middle East as part of a broader need to explain the current crisis of the Muslim world. It is particularly difficult within this context to explain Jewish or Zionist success vis-à-vis the

Muslims since, according to Islamic tradition, the Jews were destined to humiliation and subjugation to Muslims after they had rejected the message of the Prophet. It is one thing to be defeated by a superpower such as the U.S., and a completely different situation to be defeated and ruled by the Jews, who had been an inferior minority in the past under the Muslim empire, and who are a small minority in the modern Middle East. The only way to explain this cognitive dissonance is to magnify the power and evil of the Jews, and thereby help to explain Muslim weakness.[4]

Modern Anti-Jewish Animosity

The modern anti-Jewish animosity of Islamic movements goes much further than traditional Islam. Although Muslims have always viewed Islam as a superior religion, superseding Judaism, they did not consider Judaism as a heresy, which required eradication, as long as it did not challenge Islam's rule. Historically, Muslims regarded Christianity as a greater threat than Judaism, and devoted greater attention to it in their polemical literature.[5] However, due to the conflict with Israel, Judaism rather than Christianity has become the prime enemy for the Islamist organizations, drawing inspiration from anti-Jewish utterances in the Koran and from modern European anti-Semitism.

A good example of this vilification is the Hamas Charter, the movement's canonical document, which provides a picture of the Jews and Judaism drawn from the notorious anti-Semitic tract, the Protocols of the Elders of Zion. Article 22, for instance, describes the Jews as controlling the world media with their money and as having established secret organizations throughout the world—such as the Freemasons and Rotary Club—"for the destruction of societies and the fulfilment of the goals of Zionism." They have "caused revolutions all over the world," from France in 1789 to Russia in 1917 "in order to fulfil their goal." Likewise, "with their money, they seized control of the imperialist powers and pushed them to subdue many countries in order to squeeze their resources and spread their corruption." In addition, Hamas accuses the Jews of fomenting all-important wars in history. Most important, the Jews stood behind the outbreak of World War I, which "eliminated" the Ottoman Empire, the "state of the Islamic Caliphate." The break-down of Islamic unity opened the way for the establishment of "the Zionist entity" in Palestine. Likewise, they "were behind World War II, through which they made huge financial gains by trading in armaments, and paved the way for the establishment of their state."

Of special significance are the wars, which the Jews have waged against Islam from the time of the Prophet. Accordingly, the Jews op-posed the Prophet from the moment he arrived in Medina, in a desper-ate effort to prevent the spread of Islam, rejecting his generous offers and distorting his message. They tried to harm the Islamic *umma* (na-tion) and dominate it."[6]

Derogatory Descriptions of the Jews

In many of its publications Hamas employs harsh derogatory descrip-tions of the Jews, often taken from the Koran, such as "blood suckers," "brothers of apes," "killers of the prophets," "human pigs," and war-mongers "the descendants of treachery and deceit," "butchers." They are a "cancer expanding" in the land of Palestine, "threatening the entire Islamic world." They are "spreading corruption" in the land of Islam. "Deceit and usury are stamped in their nature," and they are all "thieves, monopolists, and usurers."[7]

Almost every issue of the Hamas organ, *Filastin al-Muslima* con-tains articles enumerating the evil deeds and character of the Jews based on an analysis and exegesis of specific *suras* (chapters) from the Koran.

Particularly significant, in view of the historical record, are the equa-tions, which Hamas makes between the Jews, the Zionists, and the Na-zis and the denial of the Holocaust. Hamas argues that Israel's actions exceed those of the Nazis, and that "the Jews represent Nazism in its most criminal form."[8] Yet, following the Stockholm conference on the Holocaust, held in January 2000, Hamas declared that the conference had:

> A clear Zionist goal, aimed at forging history by hiding the truth about the so-called Holocaust, which is an alleged and invented story with no basis . . . . The invention of these

grand illusions of an alleged crime that never occurred, ignoring the millions of dead European victims of Nazism during the war, clearly reveals the racist Zionist face, which believes in the superiority of the Jewish race over the rest of the nations.[9]

ᶜAbd al-ᶜAziz al-Rantisi, Hamas leader from Gaza, went further by denying the Holocaust, while simultaneously charging that "the Zionists were behind the Nazis' murder of many Jews," with the aim of intimidating and forcing them to immigrate to Palestine. Furthermore, he claimed that the Nazis "received tremendous financial aid from the Zionist banks and monopolies" prior to their seizure of power and that "this great financial aid helped the Nazis build the military and economic force needed to destroy Europe and annihilate millions." "When we compare the Zionists to the Nazis," Rantisi concluded, "We insult the Nazis".[10]

Reviewing the life of the late Pope John Paul II, the Hamas weekly *al-Risala* concluded that his 1998 letter, in which he apologized to the Jews for the Holocaust, was his "greatest crime".[11]

Advocating Jihad

The perception of the conflict as a religious one brings Hamas to advocate *jihad* (holy war) as the only way to combat the Jews. Yet, in addition to practical considerations, Hamas endowed the jihad against the Jews with eschatological significance. The messianic element is relegated to secondary importance in the ideology of modern-day Sunni movements. However, because Hamas' main preoccupation is fighting a national-religious enemy, and possibly as a means to stave off calls for a compromise among the Palestinian masses, it resorts to messianic symbolism. Thus, the jihad against the Jews is a prerequisite for fulfilling God's promise to establish His rule over the earth. Citing the tradition (*hadith*) of the Saltbush, the Hamas Charter states that the final hour will not come until the day when the Muslims will fight the Jews and kill them.[12]

Lest the meaning of this passage remain unclear, Hamas author

Mukhlis Barzaq pointed to the fact that the Prophet had killed more Jews than any other infidels during his wars. The Prophet revealed in a "firmly established Tradition" how the Jews should be handled if they betray the Muslims, and he ordered his followers to carry it out without any feelings of sorrow for this "detested group". He made it clear that the fate of the Jews should be "complete killing, total extermination and eradicating perdition (*al-qatl al-tam wal-ibada al-kamila wal-fana' al-mahiq*)." Perhaps equally significant, considering its intended readership, is the editorial in *al-Fatih*, Hamas' children's publication, appealing to the children of Iraq to pray to God and ask him "O God exterminate the Jews the tyrannical the usurpers" (*Allahuma, ahlik al-yahud al-zalimin al-mughtasibin*).[13]

Possibility of Change?

Following the Israeli withdrawal from Gaza, few Hamas activists in the West Bank voiced the possibility of future coexistence with Israel and the need to reconsider some of Hamas ideological tenets. While the possibility of changes in Hamas' ideology and attitudes should not be excluded, these views represent a very small minority within the movement's ranks. Moreover, shifts of attitudes and consciousness are usually slower than political or economic changes.

Concurrently, the harsh expressions made by Hamas should not be dismissed as mere rhetoric, as they serve to inculcate a state of mind among the movement's activists and followers as well as to socialize a younger generation of Palestinians. The horrors of the twentieth century have proved too often that extreme word leads to extreme deeds.

Notes

1. Ibrahim Quqa to *al-Anba* (Kuwait), 8 October 1988; "Hiwar shamil maʿa qiyadat Hamas," *Filastin al-Muslima* [FM] (April 1990); *Ila Filastin* (February 1990); *Nida al-Aqsa* (January 1989).
2. Bernard Lewis, "The Roots of Muslim Rage," *The Atlantic Monthly* (September 1990): 47–60.
3. "Hiwar," *FM*, April 1990.
4. For the spread of anti-Jewish sentiments in the Arab world, Bernard Lewis, *Semites and Antisemites: An Inquiry into Conflict and Prejudice* (New York: W.W. Norton, 1986); Rivka Yadlin, *An Arrogant Oppressive Spirit: Anti-Zionism as Anti-Judaism in Egypt* (Oxford: Pergamon Press, 1989).
5. Bernard Lewis, *The Jews of Islam* (Princeton: Princeton University Press, 1981), p. 33.
6. "Hiwar," *FM* (April 1990).
7. See Handbills nos. 1, 2, 4, 5, 6, 8, 14, 16, 31, 33, 65, 78, 87 in Shaul Mishal with Reuven Aharoni, *Speaking stones: communiqués from the Intifada underground* (Syracuse: Syracuse University Press, 1994).
8. *The Hamas Charter* (numerous editions), articles 20, 31. Other such statements include: "the Nazism of the Jews encompasses all of them," "the Nazi Jews," "Jewish Nazism," "Nazi Zionism," in Handbills nos. 5, 6, 8, 11, 12, 13, 14, 25, and 65.
9. Reuven Paz, "Palestinian Holocaust Denial," *The Washington Institute: Policy Watch* Number 255, 21 April 2000. The original article appeared in Arabic on Hamas' official website, Palestine-info.org, and was not translated to English, presumably because the editors realized it could harm Hamas's reputation among non-Arabs.
10. Hamas weekly *al-Risala* (Gaza), 21 August 2003. See similar claims in *FM*, September 1996.
11. *Al-Risala*, 7 April 2005.
12. *Hamas Charter*, articles 13, 9, and 7. According to Islamic tradition the Jews will flee from the Muslims on that day and "when the Jew will hide behind stones and trees, the stones and trees will say O Moslems, O slave of God, there is a Jew behind me, come and kill him. Only the *gharkad* tree (saltbush) would not do that because it is one of the trees of the Jews."
13. Barzaq, *Al-wacd min al-Khaybar ila al-Quds*, Palestine-info.org, chapter 8; *al-Fateh*, no. 8 in www.al-fateh.net.

CHAPTER TEN

FEAR OF THE OTHER

Hanna Biran

As the peace process gets under way, the question arises: just who is the Jewish-Israeli society which is about to make peace with its enemies? To what extent is this society sufficiently mature to respect the different identity of another people?

The Jewish-Israeli society is one of polarization, of fissures and of divisions within its own ranks. Among its characteristics one finds a long-standing racism toward the Oriental Jewish community living within it. It is a society which is suffering from the failure of its attempts at integration, repeated from generation to generation.

The reasons for the failure to integrate diverse elements of the population living in Israel are psychohistorical and deeply rooted. In connection with this sociohistorical situation, I wish to put forward a number of hypotheses:

My first hypothesis is that the split between the *Ashkenazi* (Western) and *Sephardi* (Oriental) is embedded in the cornerstone of the society. The people of the Second *Aliya* (wave of immigration, 1904–1914), who came from Russia to settle in Palestine, left an indelible mark on Jew-

93

ish-Israeli society for generations to come. Their values were deemed preeminent: settlement on the land and manual labor. They also abandoned religion, considered to belong to the Diaspora and thus out of date. The central idea was to give birth to a new sort of Jew, the forerunner of the proud *Sabra* (native-born Israeli).

This mentality completely overlooked and even denied the fact that the people of Israel were settling into the Middle East. It was as if the Middle East with all its characteristics did not exist. From the point of view of mentality, national identity and Jewish existence itself had been created elsewhere. What we have here is the rebirth in Palestine of European Jewry with rejuvenated characteristics.

Over the years this core of mentality was augmented by characteristics deemed to be Ashkenazi — language, accent, dress, customs, music, etc. Everything symbolizing European culture was considered supreme.

This mentality created a deep barrier between those who fitted in and belonged, and the others, those who were different. The Oriental Jews were imbued with traditional religious values. Unlike the people of the Second Aliya who lived collectively, had rebelled against the parent generation and left their homes, the Oriental youth did not distance itself from its sources in such a way as to create a new path for itself.

The Oriental Jews thus had from the start no part in the new culture. Thought of as a population which had nothing to contribute from a cultural point of view, they suffered from an arrogant and separative attitude on the part of the Ashkenazi population.

My hypothesis is that a social structure whose foundations were built in this way must influence the social mentality of the here and now. Today it is hard to reach integration when there is no basic history of bringing the various elements together. Moreover, the situation was never dealt with or corrected because the reality of the problem had always been denied. This, therefore, made it easier to ignore the actual existence of the dilemma.

Oriental Jews as an Unconscious Threat

My second hypothesis is that the Oriental Jews posed an unconscious threat to the emerging society. It appears that unconscious psychological processes created divisions and prevented the possibility of integration.

In the first years of the life of the State the extremely young Jewish-Israeli society was given to processes of formation and establishment. It was not ready to incorporate differences and to accept them as part of itself. This was a society which determined clear values for itself and held onto them. The need to live according to clear definitions was a natural one for a society in the stage of being established. In addition, there was the trauma of the Holocaust which led to placing the emphasis upon military security. The slogan was: we will no longer go like sheep to the slaughter. The national identity had to be both uniform and clear.

With this background it was more natural to regard the Middle East as a place which had to be conquered rather than as a place to which one should try to feel closer, and where one should become familiar with the peoples living in it. To approach the other and to enter into a dialogue were not the first priorities in which Jews really believed.

In this context, the Oriental Jews were not conceived as a connecting link or as a bridge capable of bringing about rapprochement. On the contrary, they threatened the clear differentiation between Europeans and Levantines, between whites and blacks. Their complex identity as Jews who were simultaneously close to the Arabs as regards color of skin, the language and customs served to blur the boundaries between West and East. For the Ashkenazim, this blurring led to fear and confusion.

Because of their dread of being influenced by the Levant and becoming part of the environment, the Ashkenazi Jews rejected everything which had an Oriental flavor. For their part, the Oriental Jews, who had for so long suffered rejection and discrimination, also began to identify with these processes: they themselves started to feel inferior and to be ashamed of their origins. A society which develops instinctive fears of the other, of the one who is different, is one which builds around itself more and more walls. Everything which is different becomes dangerous and threatening. It is a society living in mental siege, in which the other is not a partner for dialogue and a source of fertilization and growth, but a frightening, often demonic enemy upon whom are projected many fantasies connected with evil, inferiority and crudity.

Superior and Inferior in the Social Order

My third hypothesis is that the need for belonging and not belonging does not facilitate integration. The Jewish-Israeli society is made up in all its layers of immigrants who were torn from their roots and had to start afresh. In this society the terminology associated with those who came first took upon itself a mythical dimension. The first to come, the pioneers and the veterans, are the Israeli aristocracy. This phenomenon is so deeply ingrained in the psychology of the society that the new immigrant is always inferior, never belongs, has not built anything from scratch, has no foundations here. This is a society where classes are created which distinguish between those with ancestral rights and the others, who do not belong.

In addition, the society underwent a change when, following the creation of the State, it shed the pioneering values now considered anachronistic. While these values were lost, the problems of belonging continued in all their severity. The criteria for belonging changed and are now divorced from the former values; belonging is now determined by economic status and by all the accompanying manifestations of this status. However, the need for people who do not belong, who will be peripheral to the society, existed then and remains today.

Now, when we look ahead to the peace process, we must also explore the difficulties of Jewish society in making peace within itself, and the derogatory attitude toward the Oriental communities, as well as toward the immigrants of recent years from Ethiopia and from Russia. This attitude also projects upon relations with the Arabs. Because they have suffered and been humiliated, the Oriental communities themselves project a derogatory attitude upon other groups, namely the Arabs. When the social order is built upon superior and inferior, masters and servants, there is no reason why the Oriental communities will desire to form relationships with the Arabs. On the contrary, they need them as a lower order on which to deposit their own inferiority and non-belonging. What this means is that the derogatory attitude toward the Oriental communities has implications on the relationships of the two peoples, the Jewish and the Arab.

The psychological phenomenon which should be examined and researched is connected with the human need that there should always be an other, someone upon whom one can cast all the evil. The less progressive and mature the society, the more it needs to maintain — within its borders but a small distance away — another society which will typify all the lowly and inferior aspects. In this way the society itself can foster the illusion that it is exalted and superior. The three hypotheses which I have raised show that we must try to make a thorough investigation of the roots, and how the seeds of current difficulties were sown many years ago.

In a television program in December 1993, Yaron London reported how in the 1950s, the years of the great immigration from Morocco, a senior journalist from the daily *Ha'aretz* went to see the immigrants in the transit camps. After his visit, this journalist claimed in an article that the North African immigrants were barbarians. The editor of the newspaper supported the article and stressed that in his opinion, selectivity should be introduced in accepting the immigration. A great commotion arose in the wake of this, in the course of which the paper tried to shed responsibility for these racist expressions.

Discrimination — Theory and Practice

In this country there have always been commotions, and debates in which racism and discrimination have been condemned. In practice, however, in spite of declarations against racism, the Oriental Jews, including those born and bred in Israel, had to bear the brunt of not insignificant blows because of their Oriental identity.

As a daughter of Oriental Jews born in Israel in its early days, I felt that I had to erase or modify a guttural form of speaking which, though correct, was considered inferior. My parents' mother tongue was Arabic and in my childhood, Arabic was the second language spoken at home. The sound of the language always made me ashamed. The world outside brought home to me that reading and writing in Arabic were inferior.

I never thought or felt that I possessed an important asset, an instrument of communication with the East. The subtle and indirect message permeated so deeply within me that, fearing to be similar to the Arabs and identified with them, I was eventually unable to take in a single word of Arabic.

This is merely a private example of a general phenomenon which was always prevalent in Israel: the need of the Jews to preserve their identity, separatism and keeping a distance from the people of the region. This phenomenon is still making its mark today, repeating itself before our own eyes day in and day out.

In a weekly television news program in September 1994, an item was broadcast on how, in Oriental neighborhoods, six high schools currently under construction will cater only for children of the Oriental communities. This differentiation between Ashkenazim and Orientals is intended to encourage the Orientals to take a higher place in society. However, such a phenomenon should be seen as a warning light, for it is perhaps a public admission of the failure of integration.

In the New Year issue of the evening paper *Yediot Achronot,* September 1994, findings from a research project by Naomi Tsion on youth from all over the country were published by Shulamith Teneh. Here is an excerpt from the article:

> The Ingathering of the Exiles, the melting pot, a united Israeli society — all these are slogans. But it transpires that Israeli youth is full of hostile and even hateful prejudice toward groups of youth which appear in their eyes to be different from them in character. The research indicates an abyss of strangeness dividing distant and polarized groups of youth like kibbutzniks, pupils from development towns, and high school pupils from the better-off north and the poorer southern parts of Tel Aviv. Here, for example, is what the kibbutzniks thought of their contemporaries from Shderot: they are street-wise, they have an Eastern accent, they dress gaudily. Their girls are cheap, their heads are full of music and shit. The youth from Shderot is also full of stereotypes regarding the kibbutzniks: they are *Ash-*

kenazim, arrogant, leftists, snobs, square, and enjoy the benefit of favoritism in the army.

Hatred of the Other

The Israel of 1994 faces the same fissures and the same barriers which have always divided its society. Accordingly, processes of uniting, merging, and integrating are not taking place. The younger generation, which has been steeped in these failures, will continue to pass them on to the next generation.

The fear of the other, the need to see him as responsible for the bad and the inferior, is a deep and archaic human fear, the roots of which are to be found in the foundations of human culture. The hostility between Jews and Arabs is only one example of the deep human need for hatred of the other. The more a society needs the other in order to attribute its own failures and weaknesses to him, the less open it is to sustain differences and to recognize its own internal barriers.

One interesting general example which helps us to realize how deep is the fear of the stranger and how strong the need to regard him as inferior, to look down on him and to hate him, can be found in the meaning of the word "barbarian." I am referring, of course, to the changes and distortion of the original meaning of the word.

According to the *Encyclopaedia Britannica,* "Barbarian is the name among the early Greeks for all foreigners, including the Romans." The word probably represents the uncouth babbling which the Greeks heard in languages other than their own. "It soon assumed an evil meaning, becoming associated with the vices and savage nature which the Greeks attributed to their enemies. The Romans adopted the word for all peoples other than those under Greco-Roman influence and domination.

In this development of the meaning of the word, we can sense that there is a psychological need to look at someone who behaves differently, speaks a different language and looks different, as inferior to oneself. It seems that all cruelty, violence and crude behavior are projected onto the stranger. In this way, one can preserve the goodness and purity of one's own identity.

I would like to relate briefly to the book *Waiting for the Barbarians* by the South African writer J.M. Coetzee. It deals with a kingdom in which rumors broke out and spread throughout the community that the barbarians were threatening the kingdom. Coetzee does not specify time or place concerning these happenings. These events could happen any place, any time. The book tells of a colonel who wanders around the borders of the kingdom, taking into captivity barbarians that he comes across. These barbarians are simple fishermen and vagabonds who do not know what he wants from them. However, the atmosphere is full of menace. Throughout the kingdom the feeling permeates that soon the barbarians will destroy their way of life. It is therefore necessary to interrogate the captives.

The irony of the story is that the more the colonel tries to suppress the barbarians in various inhuman ways, the more he himself sinks to the uttermost depths of depravity. He, who represents culture, becomes the barbarian.

Coetzee touches here upon a universal human phenomenon. This book was written long before the Intifada, but contains an exact description of the impossible dynamics of the situation in which the Israeli soldier was placed. A soldier who became a representative of the occupation was compelled to perpetrate acts which were contrary to his human values.

Fear of the Arab — who is different, the other side, the foreign, the enemy — grew stronger in the wake of the Intifada.

A Period of Transformation

It can be assumed that a society which needs barbarians who contain all the evil, will make sure that in reality it will have such people. Jews-Israelis meet Palestinians or see Palestinians on the television only in the context of disturbances and terror, or as unskilled laborers. Many Palestinians meet Jews-Israelis only as soldiers in uniform, or as employers exploiting them.

These sorts of encounters perpetuate the fear, the suspicion, the hostility, and the hatred. The society which created these sorts of encounters overlooks the fact that this type of aggressive confrontation screened on television is the consequence of years of oppression, discrimination, and occupation.

The period ahead can be one of transformation, one of transition from violent encounters perpetuating hatred and fear, to those of a different nature, facilitating dialogue and rapprochement.

The decisive question is to what extent such a change is possible and what are the ways to encourage it. Peace with Egypt did not bring real rapprochement and seeing people as stereotypes continued. Is it possible to reach different relations between the parties, relations over and above those of cold peace? Prolonged work over generations may be needed in order to make it possible to see the other through a new prism.

Rapprochement with the stranger may take place when there are mutual interests benefiting the two peoples. Change does not take place through information, preaching, or education, since social processes permeate indirectly and with an emotional power. This is what dictates our concept of the other. It is to be hoped that change will take place through joint projects in the economic and cultural fields. In these sorts of encounters, it will be possible to relate to the other with respect, to learn from him and to facilitate the development of mutual fertilization.

So as to enable such encounters to take place, each of the peoples must feel itself sufficiently mature and confident; to reach this level, there will be a need for a long period of self-growth and development.

> Quietly, quietly a sigh melts into
> the road dust near Lod a small house at the roadside echoes
>   titillating
> tones Anu-ar Anu-ar a strange
> tone at the roadside then the road
> passed by.
> The word Arab sneaks into my mind
> troubles my calm do I too
> like my friends touch the word in panic.

— *Yossi Hadar*

CHAPTER ELEVEN

THROUGH THE SQUALLS OF HATE
Arab-Phobic Attitudes among Extreme Right and Moderate Right in Israel

Sivan Hirsch-Hoefler and Eran Halperin

"Arabs are the same as animals. There is no animal worse than them."
—Rabbi Ovadia Yosef, Haaretz, March 20, 2000

I) Introduction

Scholars investigating the extreme right wing underscore the centrality of fear and hate (xenophobia) of foreigners or immigrants as one of the core elements in identifying one's self with an extreme right ideology. Moreover, xenophobia in general and anti-immigrant attitudes in particular have been found to be key factors in explaining support for extreme right-wing parties in Europe (Lubbers and Scheepers, 2000,

2001; Lubbers, Gijsberts and Scheepers, 2004). Furthermore, the most comprehensive classification of extreme right-wing ideological features found xenophobia to be one of the five ideological components common enough to be cited by at least half of the authors in the field (Mudde, 1995).

In the attempt to fight against xenophobia, hate and discrimination, the Israeli state's Declaration of Independence emphasizes the intention to establish a society free of hatred—a society where all citizens enjoy equal rights. Yet, 57 years after its establishment, the country is still marked by hatred towards distinct minority groups, particularly the Arabs, who are hated especially in relation to the Palestinian-Israeli conflict (Yishai & Pedahzur, 1999). Similar to the European arena, xenophobia was also found to be a major factor in the ideology of extreme right-wing political parties in Israel (Pedahzur & Perliger, 2004; Sprinzak, 1991). However, given the prolonged conflict with the Arab world, it seems that xenophobic attitudes and views towards Arabs have long been pervasive in Israeli culture, and not only among right-wing extremists. In addition, the extreme right-wing label in Israel is applied exclusively within the context of the Arab-Israeli conflict, and mainly with respect to the question of the Israeli occupation of Palestinian territories. The extremist label is assigned to parties that advocate particularly hawkish positions in regard to the Arab-Israeli conflict and endorse the annexation of territories occupied after the Six Day War (Peled, 1990).

We would like to empirically examine the claim that Arab-phobia (xenophobia towards Arabs), despite its wide prevalence among Jews in Israel, can still be asserted to be a core factor in explaining extreme-right identification. In order to emphasize the role played by Arab-phobia in identification with extreme right ideology it should be analyzed vis-à-vis a close political family of the moderate right. A subsequent question therefore is whether Arab-phobic[1] attitudes can be seen as a factor that distinguishes between the extreme right wing (ERW) and the moderate right wing (MR) in Israel. We shall answer this question by examining the extent of Arab-phobia in contemporary Israel, and compare Arab-phobic attitudes of citizens who identify themselves on the extreme right of the political spectrum with those of citizens who identify themselves on the moderate right of the political spectrum. In order to make this comparison, we compiled data from four surveys, with a total number of 4,105 participants, throughout the four years of the Intifada (from September 2001 till May 2005).

II) Arab-Phobia—Conceptual Framework

Negative perceptions and attitudes towards minorities have been known for many years to be one of the main challenges facing the majority of democratic societies (Sullivan & Transue, 1999). As for the Israeli-Arab conflict, it wouldn't be too novel an idea to claim that the role of mutual and well-rooted negative attitudes and perceptions regarding members of the out-group may have enormous implications on the ability to strive towards potential solutions to the conflict (Bar-Tal & Teichman, 2005).

Conceptually speaking, the term *xenophobia* reflects an approach that views attitudes and behavior towards out-groups as mainly deriving from the challenges posed by out-groups to in-group values, identity, culture, and even socio-economic status (e.g., Lubbers & Scheepers, 2001; Mudde, 1995; Watts, 1996). Hence, we submit that xenophobia is a *"negative attitude toward, or fear of, individuals or groups of individuals that are in some sense different (real or imagined) from oneself or the group to which one belongs"* (Hjerm, 1998, p. 341). In adaptation to the terminology of the internal situation in Israel, and more specifically to the attitudes of the majority group of Jews towards the minority group of Arabs, we shall define the phenomenon as "Arab-phobia," meaning the xenophobia of Israeli Jews toward Arabs within Israel (Palestinian citizens of Israel).

The term Arab-phobia seems to have some fundamental qualitative advantages from the perspective of the current analysis. First, due to its competitive basis (out-group vs. in-group), it is very suitable to a situation where there is a genuine conflict of interests, as the one experienced by both Jews and Arabs in the last two centuries. Second, it is a most parsimonious and concise concept that unifies different cognitive and psychological aspects and in this fashion accurately reflects the generalized negative relation of the members of one group towards another. We claim that the integration of several different components, i.e., perceptions of threat, social distance, and political/social exclusion-ism, into one globalized concept may be the best reflection of a global and steady negative attitude toward minority group members. In this sense, it would be of special interest to figure out whether the concept of Arab-phobia is capable of distinguishing between moderate right-wing identification and extreme right-wing identification in Israel.

Method

Data: Public opinion data was collected over a period of four years as a part of the "Extremism Project" of the National Security Studies Cen-ter at the University of Haifa. Data consisted of four similar (but not identical) large-scale telephone surveys. Each survey addressed a rep-resentative sampling of the Israeli adult population. Survey sizes were: n=1008 in September 2001; n=1035 in February 2003, n=1016 in May 2004; n=1046 in May 2005. For the purposes of the current study, only responses of Jewish participants, who comprised approximately 80 per-cent of each sample, were taken into account.

Measures: The global concept of Arab-phobia was operationally examined according to the following three well-established scales: 1. *Threat perception* was measured by the "*national perceived threat scale*," which is commonly used in "political tolerance" studies in Israel (Sa-giv-Shiphter & Shamir, 2002). It consists of three items and yielded an Alpha Cronbach[2] of .86–.90. 2. *Social distance* was measured by the classic "social distance scale" (Bogardus, 1959), which was previously adapted and validated in Israel (Pedahzur & Yishai, 1999). It consists of four items and yielded an Alpha Cronbach of .80–.84. 3. *Exclusionism:* This variable was measured according to Scheepers and his colleagues' (2002) scale for "ethnic exclusionism" that was previously tested mainly in European countries. The scale consists of four items and yielded an Alpha Cronbach of .77–.78).

In addition to the above eleven questions measuring Arab-phobia, participants were asked to fill out a basic socio-demographic question-naire. For the specific goals of this study, participants were also asked to choose the most suitable subjective definition of their political stance.

The five options were as follows (in parentheses are the percentages of participants who chose each answer after totaling all four surveys): 1. extreme left (1.79%). 2. left (22.28%). 3. center (36.06%). 4. right (35.39%). 5. extreme right (4.48%).

Similarity and differences in support for Arab-phobic attitudes among the extreme right wing and moderate right wing

Table 1: Means (SD) of support for Arab-phobia indexes, September 2001–May 2005

2005	2004	2003	2001	Arab-phobia measurements
3.84 (1.63)	3.73 (1.76)	3.77 (1.67)	—	*Threat perception*
4.06 (1.53)	4.19 (1.57)	4.13 (1.58)	4.16 (1.63)	*Social distance*
3.77 (1.45)	3.91 (1.50)	3.82 (1.54)	—	*Exclusionism*

Note: Threat perception attitudes and exclusionism attitudes were not measured in the 2001 survey. All results refer to Jewish Israeli adults.

Looking at the whole picture, Table 1 demonstrates the scope of Arab-phobia among Israeli Jews in general. We can see that, despite enormous changes in the objective environmental situation during four years of the *Al-Aqsa Intifada*, the three measurements display a relatively high level of stability over time. Throughout the whole period, Israeli Jews presented high levels on all three components of Arab-phobia, meaning that Israeli Jews perceived Arabs as a huge threat, displayed high levels of social avoidance, and eventually supported active political acts against them. These findings illustrate that, as expected, Arab-phobia is well rooted within Jewish society in Israel. In the following stage, we used variance analysis to examine the differences between the two groups of respondents (RWE versus MR) in regard to each of these indexes.

Table 2: Means, standard deviations, and f-tests of Arab-phobia indexes according to the two groups of identification (extreme right and moderate right)

Arab-phobia measurements	2001 ERW		2001 MR		F	2003 ERW		2003 MR		F	2004 ERW		2004 MR		F	2005 ERW		2005 MR		F
	M	S.D	M	S.D		M	S.D	M	S.D		M	S.D	M	S.D		M	S.D	M	S.D	
Threat perception						5.17	1.17	4.28	1.55	14.56***	5.29	1.25	4.26	1.65	12.70***	5.21	1.30	4.54	1.39	6.15*
Social distance	5.57	.82	4.74	1.29	12.63***	5.46	.83	4.65	1.29	17.97***	5.58	.85	4.82	1.22	12.96***	5.44	.88	4.69	1.29	9.16**
Exclusionism						5.28	1.16	4.38	1.33	19.00***	5.58	.63	4.53	1.33	21.13***	5.15	1.24	4.45	1.18	9.09**

p<.05, p<.01**, p<.001***

Note: Threat perception attitudes and exclusionism attitudes were not measured in the 2001 survey. All results refer to Jewish Israeli adults.

Table 2

As seen in Table 2, significant differences were found between the two groups in terms of all measurements in the expected direction. The strongest and most significant differences were found in the exclusionism index. Although both groups demonstrate high levels of support for active political acts against Arabs, the extreme right wing exhibits much higher levels of support. In contrast, the lowest significant difference was found in the threat perception index. These findings reinforce the significance of Arab-phobia in general, and the exclusionism measurement in particular, in the distinction made between identification with extreme right versus identification with the moderate right in Israel.

Interesting findings were also discovered in the evaluation of results relating to single statements of Arab-phobia. First, there was a broad consensus among Israeli Jews—regardless of their political views or identification—in reference to two statements (at least 86% of agreement): "To what extent would you *not* agree to a member of your family having a romantic relationship with an Arab?" (Social Distance measurement). This indicates that the disinclination towards a romantic relation with an Arab is a feeling shared by most Israeli Jews, regardless of their political identification. In the same manner, regarding the statement, "Israeli Arabs endanger the Jewish character of the State of Israel", we found that Israeli Jews in general perceived Israeli Arabs as a threat to the Jewish character of the State. At no point did Jewish support for this item decline below 54 percent. However, considerable differences between extreme right and moderate right were found in reference to the other two statements of perceived threat (i.e., threat to democracy and threat to state security).

A second interesting set of findings was discovered when drawing a comparison between the results regarding certain statements within the exclusionism scale. Differences between ERW and MR exclusionary attitudes were found to be significant, with the exception of the statement dealing with non-loyal Arabs ("Arabs who are not loyal to the State should have their citizenship revoked"). It seems that the general Jewish public in Israel supports revoking the citizenships of Arabs who are not loyal to the State (83 percent in each of the surveys). However,

significant differences between ERW and MR on other exclusion statements reveal that while the moderate right is willing to exclude Arabs
mainly on the basis of their loyalty, the extreme right wing is inclined
to do so just because they are Arabs with no necessary relation to their
level of loyalty.

III) Discussion

Arab-phobia is undoubtedly a common phenomenon among all seg-
ments of the Israeli Jewish public, but as demonstrated in this study, it
is also an important factor which helps to distinguish between moderate
rightists and extreme ones. As far as we know, this is the first empirical
study to compare Arab-phobic attitudes in Israel of people who identify
with the ERW and those who identify with the MR. In general, we
found that right-wing extremists tend to feel more threatened by Arabs,
try hard to avoid social relations with them, and eventually are much
more supportive of exclusionary practices against them than people
who identify themselves as moderate rightist.

Looking more closely at the comparisons within each and every
measurement adds more depth to the picture. While the differences
between the ERW and MR in their perceptions of threat are significant
but low, the differences in the measurement of exclusionary attitudes are
much higher. Therefore, we claim that the main issue that defines right-
wing extremism in the domain of attitudes towards Arabs is the predis-
position to actively support discriminatory acts against them. Hence, it
would be correct to argue that while the perception of threat is a feeling
that is widely shared by most of Israeli society, its transformation into
an operational "will to act" is still a phenomenon that resides in one
marginal group—the extreme right.

Furthermore, it appears that while both the ERW and MR share an
instrumental ideology regarding the question (and future) of the occupied territories, Arab-phobia constitutes one of the core differences
between these two groups. Arab-phobia is well rooted among the ERW
in Israel, regardless of the actual behavior or attitudes of Israeli Arabs
(for example, whether they are loyal to the State or not, as demonstrated
earlier). Hence, identification with the ERW relies not only on hawkish

political beliefs but on hate, xenophobia, and intolerance towards Arabs as well. In our view, this fact is particularly problematic in the struggle against extremism in Israeli society and politics. In contrast to the relatively flexible and changeable political context, Arab-phobic attitudes are more ingrained and enduring.

In sum, in order to truly understand and cope with the phenomenon of the extreme right wing in Israel, it is not enough to account for instrumental territorial-ideological factors, but it is also necessary to take into consideration the social-emotional perspective, mainly Arab-phobic sentiments. With this in mind, we may carefully say that extreme right leaders—including Rabbi Meir Kahane, who was expelled from the legitimate borders of the Israeli political system—succeeded in planting seeds of hate and intolerance in Jewish society that continue to flourish over the years.

References

Bar-Tal, D., and Y. Teichman (2005). *Stereotypes and prejudice in conflict: Representation of Arabs in Israeli Jewish society.* Cambridge: Cambridge University Press.

Bogradus, E. S. (1959). *Social distance.* Yellow Springs, Ohio: Antioch Press.

Hjerm, M. (1998). "National identities, national pride and xenophobia: A comparison of four Western countries." *Acta Sociologica* 41: 335–47.

Ilan, S. (2000). "Rebellious, wicked, sinners." *Haaretz*, 20.3.2000 (Hebrew).

Levine, R. A., and D. T. Campbell (1972). *Ethnocentrism: Theories of conflict, ethnic attitudes, and group behavior.* New York: Wiley.

Lubbers, M., and P. Scheepers (2000). "Individual and Contextual Characteristics of the German Extreme Right-Wing Vote in the 1990s: A Test of Complementary Theories." *European Journal of Political Research* 38: 63–94.

Lubbers, M., and P. Scheepers (2001). "Explaining the trend in extreme right-wing voting: Germany 1989–1998." *European Sociological Review*, 17(4), 431–49.

Lubbers, M., M. Gijsberts, and P. Scheepers (2004). "Extreme right-wing voting in Western Europe." In M. Gijsberts, L. Hagendoorn, and P. Scheepers, eds., *Nationalism and Exclusionism of Migrants: Cross national Comparisons*, pp. 157–84. Aldershot: Ashgate.

Mudde, C. (1995). "Right-wing extremism analyzed: A comparative analysis of the ideologies of three alleged right-wing extremist parties." *European*

Journal of Political Research 27: 203–24.

Mudde, C. (2000*). The Ideology of the Extreme Right.* Manchester: Manchester University Press.

Pedahzur, A., and Y. Yishai, (1999). "Hatred by hated people: Xenophobia in Israel." *Studies in Conflict & Terrorism,* 22, 101–17.

Pedahzur, A., and A. Perlinger (2004). "An Alternative Approach for Defining the Boundaries of 'Party Families': Examples from the Israeli Extreme Right-Wing Party Scene." *Australian Journal of Political Science* 39(2): 285–305.

Peled, Y. (1990). "Ethnic Exclusionism in the periphery: The Case of Oriental Jews in Israeli Development Towns." *Ethnic and Racial Studies* 13 (3): 345–67.

Sagiv-Shiphter, T., and M. Shamir (2002). *Israel as a laboratory to the study of political tolerance.* Tel-Aviv: The B. I. and Lusil Cohen Institute for Public Opinion Research (in Hebrew).

Scheepers, P., M. Gijsberts, and M. Coenders (2002). "Ethnic exclusionism in European countries: Public opposition to civil rights for legal migrants as a response to perceived ethnic threat." *European Sociological Review* 18 (1): 17–34.

Sprinzak, E. (1991). *The Ascendance of Israel's Radical Right.* New York: Oxford University Press.

Sullivan, J. L., and J. E. Transue (1999). "The psychological underpinnings of democracy: A selective review of research on political tolerance, interpersonal trust, and social capital." *Annual Review of Psychology* 50: 625–50.

Watts, M. W. (1996). "Political xenophobia in the transition from socialism: Threat, racism and ideology among East German youth." *Political Psychology* 17: 97–126.

Notes

1. It is worth mentioning that Arab-phobia and Islam-phobia in general are fears that are not limited to the Israeli arena or the European scene.

2. Alpha Cronbach is the common statistical representation of the inner reliability of a scale. It measures how well a set of items measures a single unidimensional latent construct.

CHAPTER TWELVE

TO THE BONE
A Reflection on Identity

Farid Abdel-Nour

Having lived most of my life in Europe and the United States, I am accustomed to being a foreigner, to taking pride in my marginal status, and to accepting wholeheartedly the notion that identities are fluid, multiple, always in the process of being constituted. As a result, I have come to deal with identity ironically, to mock the stereotypes and ossified images with which people around me speak of Arab and Palestinian identities, and to pity their naive essentialized understandings of their own Austrian, New York, Christian, or Western identities. Today, I still have no doubt that an ironic attitude towards identity is a healthy one to adopt, especially when one directs it at oneself. Nevertheless, my visit to my childhood home in Palestine, after sixteen years of absence, taught me something important about the limits of this attitude.

My story is simple. After spending the good part of a Wednesday in Bethlehem visiting relatives, I was deposited in an unmarked illegal cab and the driver, despite my vocal protestations, was given strict orders by one of my relatives to drop me off by the Ramallah taxis at Bab il-Amood, and nowhere else. It was still early in the afternoon, and I had no intention of going back to Ramallah to be attended to and fussed over for the rest of the day by my wonderful hosts. After much cajoling, the cab driver reluctantly agreed to disregard my relative's instructions and to honor my wish of being dropped off in West Jerusalem, a previously forbidden place to me (at least psychologically). I made my way to Bab il-Khalil on foot, passing by neighborhoods I had never visited before, and made up my mind to go to the Jewish quarter of the Old City. I was curious.

Passing Unnoticed

I had anticipated being stopped, questioned, and harassed, so I kept my American passport within easy reach, assuming that I would need to rely on its authority frequently. As it turned out, to my shock, I blended in very well in West Jerusalem. Something about my appearance pegged me almost unambiguously as Jewish. I entered the square of the Western Wall unobtrusively and spent a while gawking greedily at the place and the worshipers.

Certainly, I had often been mistaken for a Jew before. However, whereas in the U.S. I could laugh at that, enjoy the irony of being mistaken for who I most certainly was not, in the Jewish quarter of the Old City the same error seemed to me devoid of irony. While I had long learned to examine the anti-Jewish feeling that I had grown up with, had long been accustomed to respecting, understanding, tolerating, sympathizing with, enjoying the company of, and looking forward to normal neighborly relations with Jews and Israelis, I was nevertheless deeply troubled by the idea of the Jew as self.

Why would such an idea have been so troubling to me? During my trip I was to return to the Jewish quarter several times. Partly in order to enjoy some moments of anonymity and inconspicuousness, but I could not bring myself to be comfortable in it. I could not like it—no matter how welcoming and accommodating it had been to me. I could not help but view it with a (perhaps maliciously) critical eye. I kept noticing how artificial, contrived, sterile, and museum-like it seemed when contrasted with the bustling Arab parts of the city, where people's everyday activities lent to the shrines an air of being incidental. It gave me comfort to view the Jewish quarter in this way. On the one hand, I still cannot shake off this impression of that quarter as a shrine in which some people have the misfortune to live. On the other hand, a part of me recognizes a little too much pleasure, too much malice in this observation. It too conveniently serves the purpose of drawing a clear line between self and Jew.

The Haram: A Visceral Experience

After spending several hours in the Jewish quarter, I made my way to the Haram. A secular person through and through, I wanted to enter the Haram for the same reason I had wanted to enter the square of the Western Wall—to gawk. It was evening by then, almost sunset, and the same thing that had rendered me inconspicuous among Jews was making me stick out like a sore thumb among my fellow Palestinians. I was stopped at Bab il-Magharbeh and informed in English that during evening prayer time the Haram was closed to non-Arabs. When I responded with great indignation and in Palestinian-accented Arabic that I *am* an Arab, the guard became apologetic, asked me a few polite questions about where I was from, and ushered me in.

I was not prepared for this way of experiencing the Haram. It was devoid of tourists. There were no less than three separate children's soccer games. Small groups were huddled in corners having what sounded like ordinary conversations (that may or may not have had anything to do with religion). Families and groups of families were finishing up their picnics under the giant cypresses. Some individuals were sitting and reading; others were engaged in calm conversations. The Haram, I discovered in one glance, is literally a sanctuary where people come to engage in the more thoughtful, reflective, and relaxed activities of their day. It seemed that, paradoxically, the Haram functions best as a public space when the public's access to it is restricted.

Unlike public spaces like Vienna's Stephansplatz, New Jersey's malls, Salt Lake City's Temple Square, or San Diego's Balboa Park, the space of the Haram seemed to induce reflection and thoughtful interaction.

We are drawn to public spaces by a complex set of desires and needs of which only variations on the desire to consume are fulfilled in commercial spaces, and of which only the impulse to indulge in self-absorption or competitive play are fulfilled in the recreational spaces of European and American parks. The Haram seemed to me at that moment to be more serious, more demanding, and to address the residual needs and desires left frustrated by malls and parks.

I left the Haram that evening knowing that I had never experienced an open space so fully, so viscerally, and that before I left the region I had to experience it in this way again, that is when it is being used, not visited. No longer interested in gawking, I wanted to be in the presence of a space that facilitates and encourages those ordinary human activities that are increasingly shut out by the world I know. I was of course being somewhat unreasonable. I myself was not using the space but visiting it. Nonetheless, I wanted it devoid of my kind. Determined to selfishly absorb more of the atmosphere of the Haram in use, I chose Friday for my next visit. Old Jerusalem's streets on a Friday soon after the noon prayer are like gushing rivers of people. That day it was as if a faucet had been opened in the Haram and people were pouring out of it at a fast pace in all directions. The sheer numbers and speed of this human traffic as well as its singular source were astounding and immediately made clear to me that, during the many years that I had lived in Palestine, I must have never visited Jerusalem on a Friday. My life in Ramallah had been strictly segregated in a largely Christian neighborhood. In retrospect, it was clear that, although I went to school in Jerusalem, I had circulated in one small area of the Old City between Bab il-Amood, Haret Innasarah and Bab il-Jdid. In other words, not only did I blend in nicely in the Jewish quarter, but I had always been removed from the rhythms of life in most of Arab Jerusalem.

An Experience of a Different Kind

Entering the Haram on Friday was a little more complicated. The guard was not as easily convinced. Even the Arabic name and Arab city of birth embossed on my American passport seemed insufficient. I looked too suspicious. Yet, somehow he acceded and allowed me in. While at first I was pleased with the apparent friendliness with which I was received by the crowds of worshipers; that is, while I enjoyed the friendly taps on the back accompanied by *"assalamu 'alaykum,"* it quickly transpired that I was the sole recipient of this effusive warmth by strangers. I was being tested. My *"wa 'alaykumussalam"* was being examined for hints of foreignness. The degree to which my presence was conspicuous, however, only became clear to me when a man with whom I had had a short casual conversation on Wednesday came up to me and apologized for the trouble I had been given at the entrance. Apparently, the guard's sudden willingness to let me in at Bab il-Sbat was triggered by a wireless conversation with this man who had assured him that, having talked to me two days before, I was so to speak "kosher."

The Haram seemed very different on Friday. People seemed to be moving with far more determination towards the entrances to the mosques and many more were in a hurry to go back home after performing their religious duty than lingering to socialize. The Haram as a public space it turns out has a fragile, periodic existence. It only functions in that capacity for a few moments every weekday when the tourists are kept at bay and the worshipers pray at home.

In one of the most surprising moments of that day, the same man came back and this time, after the usual greetings and apologies, informed me that the sheikh and the head of the guards would be interested in meeting me. Of the thousands who walked in and out of the Haram that Friday I had been singled out, watched, discussed, and it had clearly been determined that I warranted closer examination and probing. At the center of this hoopla was the question of "who I am."

One of Them?

I was led into a small room that forms part of the arcades and low walls that define the space around the Dome of the Rock and was introduced to the head of the guards, a small elderly man, wearing a *hatta*, whose no-nonsense manner was a little gruff. The sheikh, in his early middle age, was extremely tall and majestic looking; he was wearing a cream-colored tunic that accentuated his dignified demeanor. With the exception of an elderly man to my right, the ten to twelve other men

who were in the room were young and stood informally. My interrogation ensued. Where was I from? For how long had I lived in America?
What towns were my parents from?   Where did they flee to in 1948?
Where was I staying in Ramallah? Exactly which street? What did I
do for a living? What was my highest degree of education? And, finally,
getting closer to the heart of the matter, "Are you a Muslim?"

When I answered that, although I was born into a Muslim family,
I myself was secular and not a practicing, the interrogation came to a
sudden, effusive, and, to me, surprising end. Friendly slaps on my back,
smiles, probing personal questions. Was I married? Why not? Should
the sheikh take it upon himself to set me up with someone? Soon the
room emptied. I who had been picked out of thousands was no longer
special, but one of "us." Only one person seemed still interested in me:
the elderly man to my right. Since I was a "big doctor" in America,
perhaps I could help him. His son is in an American prison. Would he
receive justice in America? He offered me a cup of coffee in his room.
In his small, dark, damp room he climbed on the one chair to reach a
box in which photographs and Arabic as well as English newspaper
cuttings were piled. After listening sympathetically for a little while,
glancing over some of the cuttings of his son's arrest and trial, and explaining that there was little in my power I could do, that my expertise
did not lie in the law, and after subjecting the poor man to some plati-
tudes about maintaining hope in the face of adversity, I made my way
out of the Haram.

The Indelible Marks of Identity

The question that continued to preoccupy me for a long time after is
this: What was it that transformed me from a suspect to a confidant,
from an intruder to a brother? Something in my understanding of
religious identity was turned upside down by this experience. Was it
not one of the great innovations of the three monotheistic religions to
render birth irrelevant in the face of God? Was not the point that we
each individually tend to our salvation in our faith and actions? Was
not religion as a result a matter of individual responsibility? Does our
rejection or neglect of our religion not determine all, no matter what

our birth? Would not a secular, non-believer's damnation be as certain whether he's been born a Muslim, a Christian, or a Jew?

Schooled in the Western canon of political thought, I am accustomed to leaning on John Locke's *Letter Concerning Toleration* in many matters pertaining to religion. Locke had managed to make a case for toleration, which is all I have wanted out of religion for a long time. After my Haram experience, however, I have come to recognize what a devious trick Locke had played by focusing on the question of salvation. He ignored and repressed much about religious identity that is not quite as salutary to religious toleration. Clearly that afternoon my salvation was not at issue. What was at issue was my birth. My interrogators at the Haram were certainly aware of the existence of Muslim believers and nonbelievers, Muslims who are deserving of punishment and hell and others of honors. Their reaction tells us that my interrogators knew that among the thousands of worshipers who came in and out of this holy sanctuary on any particular Friday some are destined to be saved and others burnt. They do not make it their concern to look into the heart of each. What mattered in my interrogation was not the status of my faith or the prospects for my salvation, but my birth. I may be saved or damned, but was I a brother?

Birth marks one, sullies one, making all of one's differences from those who share the same birth differences within the family. This all seems very rigid and old-fashioned—to some even dangerous. But, can I laugh at it? Can I, brandishing Locke, dismiss my interrogators' concerns? The answer is that I cannot. My experience at the Haram, just like my critical view of the Jewish quarter, uncovers the limits of my ironic attitude towards identity. What my interrogators seem to have needed was exactly what I offered them; an assurance that I was marked. But, why did it matter? If their concern were security-based, then certainly my word ought not to have sufficed. If their concern was protecting the sanctity of the place, then would not a secular Muslim's presence defile the place as much as that of a non-Muslim? There is another possibility however. Whether consciously or not, they may have needed an assurance that, in their midst, not be one who can eye them with an outsider's gaze.

My interrogators were not only protecting the space. Under the language of security, sanctity and ritual purity, buried in their mandate for protecting the place lies a mundane worry—namely, that of having in their midst, at times of prayer, persons who may be suppressing a snicker, a shake of their head, or ones who silently murmur in their hearts "Look at them! Look at these Muslims!" Perhaps my interrogators sought to guard their community against this awful form of disregard. Perhaps they needed the assurance that I would not manifest towards them the kind of malice which came so easily to me in the Jewish quarter. Muslim birth may not be necessary to protect against this gaze, but it is sufficient. There is a way, in other words, in which vulgar birth identity cuts to the bone—an upsetting revelation to be sure, but one that I can no longer shake off.

Based on the author's diary entries in June 1999.

CHAPTER THIRTEEN

LEARNING ALL THE WRONG FACTS

Akiva Eldar

A study of Israeli and Palestinian textbooks shows how both sides tell the narrative of the conflict from their own perspective, ignoring the other side.

Israeli politicians periodically cite Palestinian textbooks as damning proof that the Palestinians are continuing to educate to hatred and not to peace. The last one to do so was Prime Minister Ariel Sharon, who called for making the curriculum the acid test of the new Palestinian leadership. The Fatah movement's candidate, Mahmoud Abbas (Abu Mazen), picked up the gauntlet, but immediately threw one of his own at the Ministry of Education: You want to examine our education for peace? Help yourself, but based on the principle of reciprocity, we should also see what's happening on the Israeli side.

It isn't at all certain that on this test the Israeli education system would get a higher grade than its Palestinian neighbor. Although it is hard to find in Israeli textbooks incidences of blatant incitement, as is often found in Jordanian and Egyptian textbooks, Dr. Ruth Firer of Hebrew University, one of the pioneers of textbook research, argues that the indoctrination in the Israeli books is simply more sophisticated.

For this reason, she says, the messages penetrate all the more effectively. It is harder to detect a stereotype that is concealed by a seemingly innocent icon, she says, than one that is worded such that it "vulgarly pulls you by the nose."

Findings of a study she conducted together with Dr. Sami Adwan of Bethlehem University, who specializes in peace education and human rights, recently appeared in a book published by the Georg Eckert Institute for International Textbook Research in Germany, entitled *The Israeli-Palestinian Conflict in History and Civics Textbooks of Both Nations*. The study encompassed thirteen Israeli textbooks (2,682 pages) and nine Palestinian textbooks (1,207 pages), and revealed a sort of mirror image in which each side pins responsibility for the violence on the other.

What the Israeli books call "events," the Palestinian ones call "uprising"; the 1948 war in the Israeli textbooks is the "War of Independence," and in the Palestinian books, *al Nakba* (The Catastrophe). Israeli textbooks regard Palestinian nationalism as a political reaction to Zionist and British policy, whereas textbooks in the territories see Palestine as a nation existing of its own accord that is at the same time part of the Arab and Islamic world.

Even though they were published after the Oslo Accords, the Palestinian textbooks emulate those in Jordan and Egypt, which have avoided use of the term "State of Israel" in texts and maps.

"In Palestinian eyes, the core of the conflict is over the land; for the Israelis, it is over security," Firer and Adwan write. "The Palestinians claim to be the descendants of the Canaanites, and thus being indigenous to the land, while the Israelis regard the Palestinians as a new nation of the 20th century born in response to the Zionist repatriation and the British Mandate. According to the Israeli version, the Israelis have rights to the land because of their religious, historical and cultural legacy. The national self-image of the Israelis includes all the layers of the past, starting with the ancient Hebrews, to the suffering Jews in the Diaspora, the victims of the Holocaust and the revived modern Jew in the Zionist Renaissance."

Almost absolute parallels

Surprisingly, the two researchers found an almost absolute parallel between the books in three areas: Both sides ignore periods of relative calm and coexistence between the nations—for instance in 1921–1929—or mention them as a misleading interval in a prolonged conflict; the two sides do not reveal any tendency to tell the pupil the story of the conflict from the enemy's point of view; both skip over details of the human suffering of the other side; and each side gives a reckoning of its victims alone.

Firer marks 1995 as the year in which a change for the good took place in peace education in Israel and quotes from a statement made by education minister Yossi Sarid in January 2000 that he had given instructions to purge from the textbooks any hint of anti-Arab stereotypes and to initiate a free discussion of less positive events in Israeli history.

The current period, since the outbreak of the Al-Aqsa Intifada and the Likud's return to power, is characterized, she says, by a retreat to the traditional educational values that emphasize love of the homeland, marginalize peace education, and abandon any attempt to understand the Palestinian side.

The chairman of the Pedagogical Secretariat at the Ministry of Education, Professor Yaakov Katz, does not claim that the Israeli education system is trying to put the pupil in the shoes of the enemy-neighbor, nor is there any reason to expect this to happen. "As opposed to critics who wish to highlight the Arab-Palestinian narrative, the education system in Israel intentionally emphasizes the Jewish and democratic identity of the state."

Katz notes that this attitude does not rule out the narrative of the other or the civil rights granted to the other by virtue of the Declaration of Independence and Israeli law.

"It would be interesting to know if there is any other place in the world in which textbooks present the narrative of the other at a time that the violent struggle between two peoples has not yet ended," says Katz. "No one should expect the democratic Jewish state to suggest during a war that it relate to the enemy's narrative in egalitarian fashion. Even more so after the Oslo Accords, about which there is a consensus that they did not bring about the yearned-for peace between Israel and the Palestinians."

Middle East History lecturer Dr. Eli Podeh of Hebrew University, author of *The Arab-Israeli Conflict in Israeli History Textbooks, 1948–2000*, expresses his reservations at the very comparison between the Israeli textbooks and those published by the Palestinian Authority.

Podeh says that while Israel is already situated in the third generation of textbooks, the Palestinians are still stuck in the first generation, which somewhat resembles the Israeli curriculum enlisted during the years of armed struggle and the initial years of statehood.

In his first study of textbooks, which was issued seven years ago, Podeh wrote, "Recognition of the important role that textbooks played in assimilating negative stands toward the Arabs has not yet been absorbed by Israeli society. This role constituted a primary factor in exacerbating the conflict in the past, and it serves as a factor that makes reconciliation difficult."

Podeh says that since then, a noticeable improvement has been made in the history books, so much so that many of them expressly note that Israel participated in deporting Arabs.

Podeh says that if the Palestinian textbooks were compelled to go through the lengthy and exhaustive process of demythologization that Israeli textbooks went through, "then the road to mutual reconciliation is, I regret to say, liable to be a long one."

Professor Daniel Bar-Tal of the Tel Aviv University School of Education, who analyzed the contents of all 124 textbooks—from grades 1 through 12, covering the subjects of literature, Hebrew, history, geography, and citizenship, all of which were approved in 1994 for use in the Israeli education system—found that the presentation of Arabs in dehumanizing terms, which declined in the 1980s and 1990s, began to seep back into the education system after the outbreak of the intifada.

He terms this phenomenon "part of the ethos of the conflict that spreads in societies subject to a violent conflict."

Like Podeh, Bar-Tal also noticed a perceptible decrease in the measure of delegitimization of the nationalistic positions of the Palestinians, but that at the same time, there has been no change in use of negative stereotypes that present the Arabs as "primitives," "passive," "cruel," or "riffraff."

Nazareth is not on the map

Dr. Nurit Peled-Elhanan of the Hebrew University School of Education recently completed an in-depth study of six Israeli textbooks published in the past few years. Some of them received official approval by the Ministry of Education's curricular division, while others were adopted by numerous teachers even without ministry approval.

One of the prominent findings in her study is the blurring of the Green Line. The book *Israel—Man and Expanse*, published by the Center for Educational Technology, features a map of Israel's institutions of higher learning, with colleges in Ariel, Elkana, Alon Shvut, and Katzrin, along with colleges in Safed, Jezreel Valley, and Ashkelon. No border is demarcated, nor is any mention made of a single Palestinian university. Nor do the book's maps show Nazareth or any other Arab city in Israel, although holy sites in the West Bank are presented as an integral part of the State of Israel.

A chapter on the ultra-Orthodox community states that they live in settlements that were established specifically for them: Kfar Chabad, Emmanuel, Elad, and Beitar Illit. The message, says Peled-Elhanan, is that the settlements are an inseparable part of the State of Israel.

On most of the maps appearing in the books examined by Peled-Elhanan, Ariel and Katzrin are marked as part of the State of Israel. A map of the national parks shows no sign of a Green Line, but does show Ma'aleh Efraim. Peled-Elhanan contends that this is merely a sophisticated way of ensuring that the pupil will espouse certain basic political assumptions.

"When the Palestinians write 'Palestine' on the maps in their textbooks, it is considered incitement," she says. "If that is the case, what should we call Israeli textbooks that call the West Bank 'Judea and Samaria,' even on maps that describe the Mandatory borders, when the official name was 'Palestine-Eretz Israel?'"

For instance, the jacket of the book *Geography of the Land of Israel* (by Talia Sagi and Yinon Aharoni, Lilach Books), a textbook that is especially popular with teachers, features a map of the Greater Land of Israel, without a trace of the territories that were already then under the control of the Palestinian Authority.

"This provides a hint to the pupil that these territories were 'ours' from time immemorial, and reinforces the message that in the Six-Day War, we 'liberated' or 'redeemed' them from the Arab occupier," writes Peled-Elhanan in her study.

Another map, in which the West Bank is marked with a different color, states that "Following the Oslo Accords, the borders of Judea and Samaria are in a dynamic process of change." The accompanying text notes that the territories of the Palestinian Authority were not marked on the map, as there is not yet any border between states.

In the case of Syria, the existence of an inter-state border that Israel does not deny does not prevent the authors from keeping it a secret from the pupil. The pupil reads that Israel annexed the Golan Heights in 1981 and applied Israeli law to it, "with all that entails." How is this supposed to influence his position on the concession of territory that had been annexed to Israel in exchange for peace with Syria? Silhouettes of two soldiers are marked on the Golan Heights; the weapon of one of them is aimed at Syria.

Professor Yoram Bar-Gal, head of the Department of Geography and Environmental Studies at the University of Haifa, says that the universal principle regarding maps used in the education realm, which states that "My map is educational—your map is propaganda," applies here in full. He says that maps are given high credibility, and therefore constitute a superior tool for transmitting political messages.

"The Zionist movement and the State of Israel, like other states and movements, have always exploited these characteristics of maps for their own needs," he says. Bar-Gal nevertheless comments that political change expressed in maps does not necessarily create change in the consciousness of teachers or pupils. "Erasure of the Green Line from the maps," he says, "did not necessarily make them disappear from the consciousness of the public at large."

Faceless refugees

Like the Green Line, the term "Palestinians" is alien to most textbooks. Until the chapter that discusses the Oslo Accords, even important historians like Professor Eli Barnavi and Dr. Eyal Naveh usually prefer the term "Israeli Arabs."

In his book *The 20th Century,* Barnavi writes in reference to the Palestinian refugees: "The longing they felt and the subhuman conditions of their diaspora" imparted "an image of the Land of Israel as lost paradise."

Peled-Elhanan points out the significant difference in his attitude toward refugees in photographs: Palestinian refugees are represented by an aerial photograph of a nameless refugee camp, devoid of any human face. This compares with a photo of Jewish refugees from Europe sitting on a suitcase in Yehud. "The Palestinian problem," the book states, "is the end result of inactivity and frustration, which were the heritage of the refugees."

Peled-Elhanan cites a series of illustrations appearing in *Geography of the Land of Israel,* which implants a camouflage message of the Arabs' primitive nature: The man in *sharwal* pants and a *kaffiyeh* on his head, the woman in traditional dress, usually sitting on the floor, and faceless children peeking from behind her back. The text explains, "The Arab resident insists on living in single-story homes, the cost of which is high. There is an expectation that all of the public needs will be provided for by the repository of land in the state's possession."

The factors delaying development of the Arab village in Israel, says the book, are that "most of the villages are situated in regions far from the center, and access to them is difficult. These villages have been left outside the process of development and change both because they are hardly exposed to modern life in the city, and because of the difficulties in linking them to the electricity and water network."

These factors do not exist when the discussion revolves to Jewish settlers who choose to settle in settlement outposts on hills that are "distant from the center, and to which access is difficult."

Naturally, Jerusalem receives special treatment in the Israeli textbooks. The book *Lands of the Mediterranean* (by Drora Va'adya, published by Ma'alot), which has Ministry of Education approval, states that "in addition to Jews," Christians and Muslims from all over the world come to Jerusalem to visit sites that are holy to each of their religions.

Peled-Elhanan comments that although the Jews are the smallest group numerically, the Christians and Muslims are annexed to them. A picture of a synagogue appears first, and it is nearly equal in size to the pictures of a mosque and a church put together. The map appended to this chapter shows Israel, including the territories, as an isolated island of Jews in a Muslim and Christian ocean, devoid of political boundaries.

In *Settlements in the Expanse,* an approved book, Peled-Elhanan found that only two lines were devoted to the history of Jerusalem from the days of King David to the modern era, whereas the yearning of the Jews for Zion was described in forty lines. The word "Arabs" does not appear at all in texts or on maps of Jerusalem: no Muslim Quarter, no Palestinian university, and no Palestinian hospitals.

Katz says that some of the criticism refers to textbooks that are not approved for use in the education system, but he is aware that certain schools do not uphold this directive. In contrast to them, the approved textbooks undergo a careful examination by experts in order to make sure that they are not contaminated by racial, ethnic, gender, or religious discrimination, and are not fraught with stereotypes.

Among the experts examining the textbooks are scholars such as Ghassem Khamaisi, the historian Dr. Benny Morris, Dan Meridor, the professors Yossi Katz, Arnon Sofer, Amnon Rubinstein, Arieh Shahar, Yossi Shelhav, and others, people who according to Katz cannot be suspected of wanting to perpetuate an imbalanced or one-sided approach.

As for maps, he says that the government's cartographic department does not mark the Green Line as an official border of the State of Israel, and that so long as the Palestinian Authority has not been recognized as a sovereign state, it should not be represented as a state on maps.

This last response is identical practically word for word with the Palestinian position, according to which marking the border will come with the permanent settlement of the border between Israel and Palestine.

CHAPTER FOURTEEN

INCITEMENT
IN ISRAELI
AND PALESTINIAN
TEXTBOOKS

Nadia Nasser-Najjab

The issue of "incitement" in Palestinian textbooks is one that has been under focus for some time now, to the extent that Israeli Prime Minister Ariel Sharon set "reform" of Palestinian school curricula as a precondition to any progress in talks with the Palestinian Authority.

Several surveys have found that there is no incitement in Palestinian textbooks, but other surveys have disagreed. The issue has raised another, parallel issue, that of similar problems in the Israeli curricula. These are not peripheral problems. A comparative analysis goes to the root of the problem of Palestinian-Israeli education, namely that the two cannot be divorced either from the realities the peoples live under and the history of the country they both claim as their own. The issue also poses the question of what education should be about: teaching the truth as it is best understood, or shaping attitudes to political circumstances.

The most recent investigation into the matter was undertaken by the Israel-Palestine Center for Research and Information (IPCRI) and was funded by the U.S. government. The report of November 2004, *Recommendations for Palestinian Text Book Reform,* was the third in a series of three evaluations of the Palestinian curriculum presented to the Public Affairs Office at the U.S. Consulate General in Jerusalem (the other two were *Analysis and Evaluation of the New Palestinian Curriculum: Reviewing Palestinian Textbooks and Tolerance Education Program (Report I)*, March 2003, and *Analysis and Evaluation of the New Palestinian Curriculum: Reviewing Palestinian Textbooks and Tolerance Education Program Grade 4 & 9 (Report II)*, June 2004. IPCRI also carried out one evaluation of Israeli textbooks, *Examination of Israeli Textbooks in Elementary Schools of the State Educational System*, April 2004.

Comparing Israeli and Palestinian Textbooks

In this article I will examine the report issued by IPCRI in November 2004 and compare its findings with the April 2004 evaluation of Israeli textbooks. The overall evaluation of the latter was positive, as best summed up by this excerpt of the report's closing paragraph:

"Our hope is that the balance will continue, the injustices requiring correction will be corrected as well as the contents of the books, and that the factual aspects will be more emphasized than the mythological aspects."

While there is some criticism of Israeli textbooks for not teaching enough about Arabs and Palestinians, there is no mention, however, in the IPCRI report of an earlier study by Professor Daniel Bar Tal of Tel Aviv University, which in 1998 found that Israeli textbooks described Arabs as "hostile, deviant, cruel, immoral, unfair, with the intention to hurt Jews." In other words, Israeli textbooks are criticized for what they leave out, but not in any way accused of incitement.

The "velvet glove" treatment afforded Israeli textbooks can be seen in other contexts as well. There is an inherent imbalance in the treatment afforded Israeli and Palestinian curricula by IPCRI when on the one hand Israeli students are implored to "be challenged to understand the period of the Oslo peace process in all of its complexities" (this in the November 2004 report), while Palestinian teachers should "place an emphasis on positive Palestinian intentions and positive elements [that] occurred during the Oslo process, such as the establishment of the Palestinian Authority".

Two examples are included in the IPCRI report on grade 2 Israeli history curriculum intended to show that it promotes a balanced view. One concerns a cautionary tale of how Jews should avoid buying land close to Arab settlements. The intention, according to the IPCRI report, is that it teaches students to maintain good relations with their Arab neighbors, but with no mention of illegal Jewish settlements in the West Bank and Gaza; to ferret out such intention rather depends on classroom discussion management by the teacher. Another, equally teacher-dependant example, concerns the biblical story of the negative impact of Philistine rule. That example, according to the IPCRI report, should show the negative impact of one people ruling another, but it is for the teacher to bring such a message out. Another message can easily be understood.

More important, for our purposes, is that while Israeli teachers are afforded the benefit of the doubt by the IPCRI report writers that they will indeed steer the classroom discussion in a "positive" direction, no similar faith is placed in Palestinian teachers, and no leeway is given equally ambivalent examples from Palestinian textbooks.

In another example, the IPCRI report criticizes the Palestinian curricula for not explicitly recognizing the right of Israel to exist. While it does include criticism of Israeli textbooks for not recognizing the 1967 borders, the writers behind the IPCRI report apparently feel this should not be a justification for the Palestinian side to do the same. A recent article on the issue by Akiva Eldar in the Israeli *Haaretz* newspaper ("Learning all the wrong facts", December 9, 2004) finds that not only is the 1967 border not recognized, the Green Line receives no mention at all and the West Bank is referred to only as Judea and Samaria.

The lack of education in the Israeli textbooks surveyed for grade 2 schoolchildren about Palestinian identity is explained away as not relevant to the period taught, while grade 4 Palestinian textbooks are taken to task for not mentioning any historical Jewish presence in the land. It seems odd to expect young Palestinian schoolchildren to learn ancient Jewish history and not for Israeli schoolchildren to learn much more recent history about Palestinians and Palestine, but it also raises questions about the methodology of the IPCRI team. Why a whole series on the Palestinian curricula and only one report on Israeli primary school curricula? Indeed, why the IPCRI recommendation to have Israeli experts on the committees to evaluate Palestinian textbooks, but no Palestinian experts to review Israeli textbooks?

The Palestinian curriculum is generally criticized for teaching animosity toward Israel. For example, the November 2004 report includes the following quote from a Palestinian textbook:

> They (the Israelis) have taken our land, they destroy our homes, they have determined our future, and the only thing we can hold onto as our own is our identity and our past. Now they want to take that as well.

Considering what is happening on the ground, it is very hard for me to see what is wrong with the above quote. Indeed, while Palestinian teachers are urged to teach the negative effects of suicide bombings on Israeli civilians, in all four IPCRI reports not one mention is made of the Israeli occupation and Israeli aggression against Palestinian civilians. The IPCRI reports seem to assume that peace has been struck, that people's rights have been met, that the occupation no longer exists. But children, as any teacher knows, will always ask awkward questions, especially when those questions are posed of them every day in the form of foreign soldiers and bulldozers, checkpoints and curfews, death and destruction.

It is singularly dispiriting to find a non-governmental organization that, by its own definition, is devoted to achieving a just peace between Palestinians and Israelis, publishing an account so devoid of balance. It is dispiriting to find this same organization in their November 2004 report urging the PA to recognize Israel as the "State for the Jewish people," thus relegating Israel's Palestinian population to second-class status, not to mention the rights of Palestinians from pre–1948 Mandate Palestine.

IPCRI challenges Palestinian educators to focus on the new period. What new period this refers to is not exactly clear. "Peace education," as some like to call it, can be very useful in fostering tolerance and understanding, but cannot come at the expense of reality. No amount of fine words will challenge the evidence of your own eyes. As settlements continue to expand, and a wall is built up and down the West Bank (perhaps equally confounding for Jewish children, up and down "Judea and Samaria"), it is simply unrealistic for IPCRI to ignore these factors. If we are to learn about the Oslo process "in all its complexity" perhaps we need to learn why it hasn't brought peace.

CHAPTER FIFTEEN

THE ARAB IMAGE IN HEBREW SCHOOL TEXTBOOKS

Daniel Bar-Tal

This article examines the representation of Arabs in Israeli Jewish education. Specifically, it reviews studies on the curriculum in textbooks used in the elementary and secondary Israeli Jewish schools, pointing out the changes that took place in different periods. This review is important because school textbooks provide an illustration of the shared societal beliefs, especially in democratic societies. That is, they constitute formal expressions of a society's ideology and ethos, its values, goals, and myths (Apple, 1979; Bourdieu, 1973; Luke, 1988). The above implies that school textbooks do not provide neutral knowledge, but rather construct a particular societal reality, particularly in language, literature, history, geography, religious studies, civic studies, and social sciences. The selection of the "knowledge" to be included in the textbooks is a political process, and subject in some states to official approval.

The knowledge imparted through textbooks is usually presented and perceived as objective, truthful, and factual. Down (1988), from the Council for Basic Education in the U.S.A., stated these ideas very directly: "Textbooks, for better or for worse, dominate what students learn. They set the curriculum, and often the facts learned, in most subjects. For many students, textbooks are their first and sometimes only early exposure to books and to reading. The public regards textbooks as authoritative, accurate, and necessary. And teachers rely on them to organize lessons and structure subject matters" (p. viii).

I, therefore, assume that in the hundred years of the Arab-Israel conflict, textbooks played an important role in shaping attitudes towards Arabs of Jews and Israelis educated in Hebrew schools in Palestine and, later, in Israel. The first school textbooks for the children of the Jewish immigrants in Palestine were written abroad by Zionists, and only from the early 1900s were the books written in Palestine. These books were used in the schools established by the Zionist immigrants, who paid special attention to education, and almost from the beginning of the establishment of the Jewish settlement in Palestine (called the Yishuv), the educational system was institutionalized. Within a short time, the school system was divided into three trends—the workers', the religious, and the general—and this continued to operate during the British Mandate. After the establishment of the State of Israel in 1948, educational trends were unified under the supervision of the Ministry of Education in 1953, but division between non-religious and religious state schools remained (Eisenstadt, 1967). As a centralized system, the Ministry of Education had the authority to approve the use of school textbooks on the basis of curricula developed by the ministry, which outline the didactic, scholastic, and societal objectives that should be achieved (Eden, 1971).

National above Educational Goals

During the State of Israel's first twenty years of existence, national objectives were viewed as being of the highest importance in the educational endeavor. The Minister of Education, Prof. Ben-Zion Dinur, outlined these goals directly in 1953:

The position of our country must form the underlying premise of the civil education system. The State of Israel was born after a long and difficult struggle. It was established in the midst of a civil war. The struggle still continues... Officially, we are living in that vague shadowy situation which is neither war nor peace. We resemble a city under siege... We are surrounded by enemies whom we fought during the War of Independence and who have yet to reconcile themselves to our existence.... (quoted in Podeh, 2002, p. 38).

In the 1970s, the Curriculum Department of the Ministry of Education, which was established in 1966, went through a major reorganization and began to emphasize more didactic and scholastic objectives at the expense of national and societal ones. In the mid-1990s, the Ministry of Education lost its authority to control the use of school textbooks, especially in high schools, and, most frequently, the decision on what kind of books to use in a school nowadays depends on its staff. This new trend stimulated publications of textbooks, especially in history, which dared to present a "revisionist" view of the Israeli past. In the Israeli educational system, societal beliefs are transmitted through schoolbooks on history, literature and Hebrew, geography, social sciences, civic studies, and Bible studies. The following review will focus on major studies that analyzed school textbooks in history, geography, Hebrew (in lower classes which use readers), civic studies, and Arabic. It will discuss the image of Arabs that the books portray in three periods: during the pre-state period, between 1948 and the 1970s, and between the 1970s and the 1990s. This division reflects those changes that took place in the structure and objectives of the educational system.

The most extensive and comprehensive studies of history school textbooks in Israel were done by Firer (1985) and Podeh (2002). The first content study analyzed 93 history textbooks, used in the Jewish schools in Israel between 1900 and 1984, examining their role as agents for Zionist socialization. The second study analyzed 107 history and civic studies textbooks published from 1946 until 1999 to examine the presentation of the Arab-Israeli conflict. Bar-Gal (1993, 1994) wrote the most extensive study of geography textbooks, analyzing the content of 192 books published between 1894 and 1989.

The Arab in School Textbooks of the Pre-State Period

According to Firer (1985), all the history books from 1900 focused on justifying the exclusive rights of the Jewish people to the country, disregarding the rights of the Arabs to the country, and rejecting recognition of their national rights, while noting but also denying their religious rights. The books emphasized that this country, the Jewish homeland, was conquered by different peoples including Arabs, was neglected through the centuries and waited to be redeemed by Jews. In fact, Firer found that, until 1930, Arabs were rarely mentioned in the history textbooks and, when the books referred to them, they were viewed as part of the "natural disasters" with which the immigrants had to cope in building their new life. Only after 1930, as the violent conflict escalated, did there appear detailed references to Arabs, describing them uniformly as "robbers, vandals, primitives and easily incited" (p. 128). The Arabs were also portrayed as being ungrateful, since the Jews came to contribute to the development of the country, and the Arab leaders nevertheless incited them against Jewish settlement.

The analysis of geography textbooks published in Palestine by Bar-Gal (1993, 1994) showed a similar trend. He identified five characteristics in the treatment by Jewish writers of Arabs: disregard, contempt, and ethnocentrism, but also romanticism and humanity. During the first few decades of Zionist immigration, most of the geography school textbooks were written by authors who lived in Europe and treated Arabs as "invisible people." But some books, especially those by authors living in Palestine, did describe Arabs. All these perceived Arab society ethnocentrically, as was the customary European view, with a feeling of Jewish superiority. These books, like Grazowski in 1903, differentiated between different Arab sectors. But in Bar-Gal's view, all Arabs had common characteristics of backwardness and ignorance (Bar-Gal, 1994, p. 225).

Several authors of geography textbooks described Arabs in a romantic perspective, focusing on their exotic food, dress, markets, and way of life — especially the Bedouins, who were appreciated as brave warriors, proud human beings, freedom lovers, and hospitable. They were seen as reflecting the way of life of the ancient Israelites. In this context, some authors described the Arab villages as exotic places where women draw water from the wells and Arab shepherds graze their flocks in the fields. Some books express empathy and pity over the hard life of the Arab *fellahin*. All the books had the highest regard for the Druze community, because of their physical appearance, bravery, generosity, and virtues (Bar-Gal, 1993).

As acts of Arab violence increased in the 1920s, and especially in the late 1930s, the geography textbooks began to present the Arab as the enemy (Bar-Gal, 1993, 1994). Arab violence was at first viewed as a continuation of the pogroms in Eastern Europe, but later it was seen as hostility toward the Zionist goals. As in the history books, the geography books described Arabs as a "mob which threatens, assaults, destroys, eradicates, burns and shoots, incited by haters of Israel."

The Arabs in School Textbooks: 1950s–1970s

Following the establishment of the State of Israel and until the 1970s, school textbooks continued to present a very negative picture of the Arabs. In fact, they took the same ideological-educational line as textbooks in the Yishuv. Thus, according to Podeh (2002), the history textbooks written after 1948 (the "first-generation" textbooks in the State of Israel) continued to describe Arab neglect of the country because of their backwardness and primitivism, as well as their cowardice, treachery, and violence. According to Firer (1985), the first books in the State of Israel were influenced by the Holocaust trauma and used extreme words to describe the Arab role in the Jewish-Arab conflict. Most of the books failed to mention the existence of the Palestinian nation, its aspirations, or the driving force of Palestinian nationalism. The events of 1936–1939 were presented as disturbances and riots by "Arab gangs," and some books even noted Arab ties to Nazi and Fascist movements in Europe (Podeh, 2002). As one textbook wrote, among the Arabs, "inflammatory Italian and German political propaganda, which aimed at harnessing the Arab movement to the chariot of its own political interests, fell on the fertile ground of religious and national fanaticism" (quoted from Podeh, 2002, p. 120).

The 1948 war was presented as a struggle between the few (Israel) and the many (the Arabs), starting with attacks by local Arab gangs and followed by invasion by seven Arab states. The reason for the refugee problem was that the Arabs fled following their leaders' propaganda, despite Israeli attempts to persuade them to stay. For example, one text-book wrote: "The Arabs fled the country a few weeks prior to the end of the Mandate. A panic-stricken mass flight began. The spirit of the Arab population was broken and they were in a state of utter terror. Destructive and malicious propaganda only added fuel to the conflagration. The Arabs were deluded into thinking that they would soon return victori-ous to the country, expel the Jews and seize their assets as spoils of war" (quoted in Podeh, 2002, p. 129). Similarly, the subsequent Israel-Arab wars were described as acts of Arab aggression. The books spoke about Arab hatred of Jews, and their anti-Semitism as motivating forces in initiating violence (Firer, 1985).

The delegitimization of Arabs was also presented in Hebrew read-ers. In order to examine how Arabs were stereotyped, Zohar (1972) analyzed 16 elementary school readers (8 for the religious and 8 for the secular educational systems, 2 books for 2 grade levels), published and widely used in the 1950s and 1960s. First of all, she found that the Arab people were most frequently referred to as a collective, and rarely as individuals. They were mainly described in the context of conflict, either before or after the 1948–49 war. Only rarely did the books refer to Arab citizens of the State of Israel. On a general level, Arab society was presented as primitive, backward, and passive. Arab farmers and shepherds did not try to improve their condition of life or the way of farming. Their houses were described as poor, neglected, and crowded and, in some readers, their clothing was described as dirty. The secular readers provided more extensive pictures about Arab culture and life, noting positive features like hospitality, and a few books included stories about friendship between Arabs and Jews.

The Arabs as the "Enemy"

The most frequent presentation of Arabs was as "the enemy," no mention being made of their national aspiration, of the context of conflict between two national movements. Zohar (1972) concluded that the delegitimization and demonization of Arabs in the readers, and the avoidance of a human, multidimensional, and individualized approach, aimed to impart national Jewish values in times of conflict.

In many respects, the findings in the study of geography books by Bar-Gal (1993) are similar to those of Zohar. Bar-Gal found that, during the 1950s and 1960s, the books presented "the glory of the ancient past, the destruction and negligence when the Jewish people went into exile, and the renewal and revival of the landscape with the help of the Zionist movement" (Bar-Gal, 1993, p. 150). Bar-Gal noted another characteristic of geography books, namely their disregard of the tragedy experienced by the Arabs during the 1948 war when hundreds of thousands became refugees, and many Arab villages were destroyed.

However, Bar-Gal (1994) noted that, following the 1948 war, the direct delegitimization of Arabs living in the State of Israel gradually ceased. The reference to their ignorance and primitivism slowly disappeared and their description as an enemy of Zionism faded. Unlike Arabs who lived beyond the borders, and who continued to be stereotyped negatively, the books dwelt on the integration of the Israeli Arabs, called "minorities" in the Jewish-Israeli society, the Jewish contribution to their development and their good treatment by the state authorities, which built educational, health, and welfare systems in the Arab villages, bringing progress to the Arabs and introducing them to modernity (Bar-Gal, 1993, 1994).

This line of description continued in the 1970s and 1980s. A similar approach is found in geography books, dealing with the Arab population in the territories conquered in the 1967 war. For example, in one book of 1975, Rina Habaron wrote the following about the Gaza Strip: "The military government canceled discrimination between the local population and refugees and brought improvement in the areas of education and sanitation, which are provided free of charge. Health services standards were improved. Innovations were introduced into agriculture,

with the farmers receiving guidance and having their products market-
ed in the country... The Israeli Electricity Company connected up with
Gaza and established a basis for the development of new industries"
(quoted from Bar-Gal, 1993, p. 186).

However, the books also presented positive traits such as Arabs'
hospitality, their combativeness, their pride, and their habit of working hard. Also, Arabs were viewed as a heterogeneous society, which
includes different elements. Overall, however, Bar-Gal concluded that
how the Arabs were described depended on their degree of cooperation
with the Zionist enterprise. In our terms, we can say that their presentation depends on the nature of relations between Jews and Arabs, as
Jews perceive them. This ethnocentric view provided the main criteria
for their stereotyping.

The Arab in School Textbooks in the 1970s

During the 1970s, the Ministry of Education initiated a major shake-
up of the curricula, which led to changes in the content of textbooks.
The new policy diminished the role of the national objectives in design-
ing school curricula. Rather, it stressed the didactic and scholastic objectives, also taking into consideration new aspects of psychology now
available on the development and needs of pupils.

In the 1970s, descriptions delegitimizing Arabs almost disappeared
in history school textbooks (Firer, 1985). Podeh noted that during the
late 1970s, 1980s, and early 1990s, history books of the "second generation" were written — the "adolescence period." These books permitted
the acknowledgment of the existence of Palestinian nationalism, used
less pejorative terminology in the description of violent Arab resistance
to Jewish immigration and settlement, and began to present a more balanced picture of the origins of the Palestinian refugee problem (Podeh,
2002).

In 1979, the Ministry of Education published the first school textbook, *The Arab-Israeli Conflict for History and Civil Studies,* to include
original Arab documents and speeches by Palestinian leaders, including material about Palestinian national aspirations. In general, Arab in-
transigence was presented as the norm, as well as Jewish willingness to

compromise.

A similar line was taken in the second part of the book on the post-1948 period, which deals with the inter-state conflict between Israel and the Arab states. The book provided material justifying the Sinai Campaign (1956) and the Six-Day War (1967) and presenting the non-compromising positions of the Arab leaders in contrast to Israeli willingness for peace. However, it included relevant documents, some Palestinian. The two books were eventually dropped in the 1990s on the grounds that they had become out of date.

An Adult Approach

In the late 1970s, the Ministry of Education also published two new books: *We and Our Neighbors* (1979) for elementary and junior high schools, and *Living Together* for high schools. The first book described neighboring Arab countries in reconciliatory tones, and the second openly presented issues related to the Arab minority in the State of Israel. The latter book was revised and published in 1988 under the title *The Arab Citizens of Israel*. It represents major progress towards the presentation of a balanced description of the Arab citizens of Israel. It describes their life in Israel and their relations with the Jewish majority, but it is one of the few, and maybe even the only book, which openly discusses discrimination against Arabs in Israel, including expropriation of their land. This book aims to provide updated information about the Arabs in Israel and to change their negative stereotype in Israel in order to advance positive coexistence between the two groups.

The Arabs in Readers and Arabic Language Studies

In readers written in the 1970s and 1980s, a more quantitative study by Bar-Tal and Zoltak (1989) surveys the stereotyping of Arabs analyzing a sample of 20 readers approved for use in elementary schools and junior high schools in 1984. It was found that the readers devoted little space to Arabs, in spite of the fact that they constitute a substantial minority of about 20 percent of the Israeli population. With regard to the Arab image, the study found that in 50.7 percent of the items the image was negative, in 29.1 percent it was neutral and in the rest positive.

Most of the positive images were in the context of presenting individuals. Arabs were presented, for example, as "human savages," "bloodthirsty," "gangs of murderers," "infiltrators and terrorists," or "robbers."

The next study by Brosh (1997) analyzed Arab representation in the
school textbooks of Arabic language studies. In Israel, about 12 percent
of the Jewish students learn Arabic language in post-elementary schools,
the great majority of them in junior high schools. Brosh analyzed 12
Arabic language textbooks written by Jews in the 1970s and 1980s, and
used in the junior high schools. The results of his study showed that,
historically, the Arab is usually positively presented against the background of the beginning of Islam and its expansion. These are described
as people of high moral standards and religious faith. The contemporary
Arab (mostly male) is presented in two ways: traditional and modern.
The former, which is more prevalent, focuses mostly on primitive *fellahin*
and manual workers. The *fellah* is described as "a primitive laborer who
cultivates his soil in traditional ways without agricultural equipment...
resides in a tent in the village, and his main means of transportation are
the donkey and the camel... The Arab has no leisure

time. His children remain in the same backward condition and there
is no improvement or progress in the younger generation... He has a
moustache and a beard, and he wears the traditional *kaffiyah*, the Arab
headdress" (Brosh, 1997, p. 317). The modern Arabs, in contrast, "seem
to approach a Western style of life. They have cars and reside both in villages and cities... they cultivate the soil with modern agriculture equipment... watch television, and take up liberal professions" (Brosh, 1997,
p. 317).

According to Brosh, the books tend to depict the primitive side of
Arab society, without any attempt to differentiate between various religious groups. The issues and problems with which Arab society in Israel
has to cope are not presented. The descriptions of Jewish-Arab contact
are simplistic, and are not placed in the context of overall relations between the Arab minority and the Jews in the State of Israel, or between
Israel and the Arab world. Recently, Bar-Tal (1998b) analyzed the content of all the school textbooks of all those school grades (1 to 12) in
history, geography, civic studies, and Hebrew (readers), approved by the

Ministry of Education for use in schools in 1994–95 and which referred to Arabs, or to the Arab-Jewish conflict. In total, 124 school textbooks published between 1979 and 1994 (the great majority of them published in the 1980s and early 1990s) were examined. The objective of the study was to reveal the extent to which the school textbooks express societal beliefs on the ethos of conflict. For our purpose, we will concentrate only on those results pertaining to Arabs' stereotypes and especially to their delegitimization.

Textbooks in the 1980s–1990s

In general, the analysis shows that there is very infrequent direct delegitimization of Arabs (one or two references), in about 30 percent of the elementary school readers, in about 20 percent of the junior high-school readers, in about 20 percent of the secular history books, in a few geography books, and in one civic studies book. These findings don't refer to negative stereotyping. The great majority of the books stereotype Arabs negatively wherever they are referred to. Positive stereotyping is an exception.

With regard to readers, first of all it was found that most of the readers have very few stories about Arabs or Jewish-Arab relations. Even then, the references to Arabs appear in the context of the Israeli-Arab conflict, while the textual item focuses on the Jews. Most of the books, when relating to Arabs, stereotype them negatively, with a tendency to present Arabs as primitive, uneducated, passive people, without a will of their own, and as poor farmers or shepherds. The stories describing early Arab-Jewish relations during the pre-state period and after the establishment of the State of Israel are frequently of a violent nature. In all, the Arabs are portrayed as aggressors, leading to their delegitimization as a "mob," "bloodthirsty," "murderers," "inhuman enemy," or "rioters."

Nevertheless, it should be noted that the readers also contain positive images of Arabs. These are all on an interpersonal level and describe a friendship between a Jew and an Arab, or how an Arab helped a Jew. In most of these stories the Arab is presented as a low-status person. Exceptional is a story about a Jewish family visiting a middle-class, educated family in an Arab village. In a few stories the Jewish-Arab friendship ends with the eruption of hostilities. There are also a few readers, mostly for junior high schools, which present positive material from Palestine and elsewhere (some even written by Arabs) on Arabs and their way of life as individuals. Of special importance are stories that describe empathetically the suffering of the Arabs in the context of the Israeli-Arab conflict. Examples are a poem by Nathan Alterman, which deals with an incident in which a Jewish youth destroys an Arab's watermelon crop, or a story describing Arab refugees during the 1967 war.

Geography books for the elementary and junior high schools stereotype Arabs negatively, as primitive, dirty, agitated, aggressive, and hostile to Jews. One book writes, "Gloomy residents walk about the village, in poverty and silent horror... Children suffering from eye disease and with swollen stomachs wander through the garbage...." One book, *Jews and Arabs in the State of Israel,* published in 1989, approaches geography by exploring Jewish-Arab relations in contemporary Israel. In its introduction the author states, "We believe and hope that the learning, acquaintance, and meetings between you and the other [i.e., Arab] students will eventually contribute to the understanding and mutual respect between Jews and Arabs living in Israel" (p. 4). This is an exceptional book, which describes the life of Arabs in Israel, and Jewish-Arab relations also from the Arab perspective. The author expresses a view that the resolution of the conflict can be achieved through continuous and complex negotiations (p. 7).

A geography textbook for high schools, entitled *Changes in the Geography of Israel,* published in 1991, includes articles on demographic geography. Two articles present conflictual relations with Arabs and discuss the threats of their presence in the Galilee: Jewish settlement in the Galilee is said to be necessary in order to prevent the Arabs from becoming a majority in the region, to change the demographic balance of the Galilee in favor of the Jews, and to ensure Jewish territorial continuity. In another book published in 1992, *Israel: Geography of a Country,* Arabs are presented completely negatively as "an incited Arab mob" (p. 131), as "mercenary Arab gangs" (p. 190). The book also describes the progress and assistance that Jews brought to the occupied territories after the 1967 war.

The history books in the elementary schools hardly mention Arabs.

This is of special interest, since they deal with the pre-state period when Arabs were the majority in Palestine. Whenever the Arabs are noted, they are predominantly associated with aggressive behavior and with primitivism. History books for junior high schools continue to describe the aggressive and violent behavior of Arabs in the pre-state period. They are shown to oppose Jewish immigration, harass and murder Jewish pioneers, and carry out pogroms. In these books, they are sometimes labeled with delegitimizing categories such as "rioting gangs," "murderers without distinction," "Arab mob," or "violent animals." The books do present the Palestinian national aspirations, albeit in an uncompromising and extreme position. The Arab leaders reject any compromise or any peaceful resolution to the conflict. The books describe the Arab people as being forcefully agitated by an extreme leadership, which leads them to promote violence.

The history textbooks of the high schools, the majority of which cover the Arab-Jewish conflict, stereotype the Arabs negatively. Arabs are presented as intransigent and uncompromising. One book claims that the Arab hostility in the 1930s and 1940s was fed by the anti-Jewish propaganda spread by the Nazis and Italian Fascists. But only three books (21 percent) have at least one reference that delegitimizes Arabs. One book, *The Zionist Idea and the Establishment of the State of Israel*, is of special significance. Analyzing the Israeli-Arab conflict and attempting also to offer the Arab perspective, it devotes ten pages to the description based on Jewish sources of the Arab national movement. Thus, it presents the rise of this movement as the reaction to the emergence of Zionism, that is, "the fear of penetration and consolidation of the Zionist factor in the Land of Israel" (vol. 2, p. 86). The book in general presents a negative picture of Arabs as enemies who try, through violence, to stop the realization of the Zionist ideology.

It should be noted that a change of major significance with regard to history school textbooks took place in the mid-1990s. In the last few years, books of the "third generation" in the State of Israel were published: Podeh called them "books of adulthood." Many used newly released archival material, which shed a more balanced light on the Arab-Jewish conflict and allowed for more openness, pluralism, and criticism. In these books, Arabs are presented "not only as mere spectators or as aggressors but also as victims of the conflict... For the first time, there appears to be a genuine attempt to formulate a narrative that not only glorifies Zionist history but also touches on certain shadows in it. Moreover, in many cases there is no attempt to avoid discussion of controversial questions, such as the Palestinian refugee problem, Israel's presence in Lebanon, the desirability of establishing a Palestinian state, etc." (Podeh, 2002, p. 184). Many of these books refer to the Palestinian nation, recognize the role of Palestinian nationalism in the development of the Arab-Jewish conflict, describe in a balanced way the violent acts of Palestinians against Jews in periods of conflict, and provide an objective description of the wars (Podeh, 2002). In general, they provide a new perspective to the Arab-Jewish conflict, presenting a more complex and multidimensional picture of the Arabs, in general, and the Palestinians, in particular.

Stereotyping and Delegitimizing

In conclusion, it is possible to say that almost all the Israeli school textbooks that referred to Arabs in the context of the conflict have continuously stereotyped them negatively, and even delegitimized them following the Jewish experience of continuous violent confrontation with the Arabs over more than a hundred years. This conclusion is based on the finding that Arabs are mostly presented in the context of the conflict and, in this context, they are almost always negatively stereotyped.

The conflict provided a problem to the Jewish educators — how to present Arabs. It began with the first textbooks written at the end of the nineteenth century, which, if they acknowledged the existence of the Arab population in Palestine, did not recognize its national entity.

It was mainly on the pre-state period and the 1948–49 war that the delegitimizing labels appeared. The pre-state years were formative in Israeli history, when waves of Jewish immigrants were escaping from European anti-Semitism and later from the approaching Holocaust. Trying to rebuild the land and the nation, the Arabs stood in their way. This is a mythical period that serves as a basis for many of the Israeli societal beliefs. It provides the image of a pioneering society trying to found the Jewish state and at the same time defending itself. The writers focusing on the Zionist narrative do not understand why the Arabs failed to accept the Jews with open arms and violently resisted their return to their ancient homeland. This opposition is therefore attributed to the incitement of the Palestinian masses against the Jews.

Hence the 1948–49 war, to which the books devote much space, is projected as a violent Arab attempt to prevent the establishment of the Jewish state, and the longest, most decisive, traumatic, and costly war in terms of human losses. Other periods of conflict receive less attention in the books.

The question that can be asked, then, is what kinds of representation of Arabs do students find in school textbooks? The great majority of the books at best stereotype Arabs negatively, but often they also delegitimize them in the context of the conflict. From these descriptions, students can learn two major themes of Arab characteristics. One concerns their primitiveness, inferiority in comparison to Jews, backwardness, and ignorance. The other theme relates to their violence, to characteristics like brutality, untrustworthiness, cruelty, fanaticism, treacherousness, and aggressiveness. The books provide graphic descriptions of Arab pogroms, murders, and riots, the result of agitation and incitement of the Arab masses by their leaders. Arabs are usually presented as a threat to Jewish existence and this stereotype is assumed to arouse feelings of insecurity, fear, and hatred. Positive stereotyping is rare. Some of the books refer to positive characteristics, which appear mostly in a particular ethnocentric framework, whenever Arabs help Jews or recognize their superiority. Even so, some books describe Arabs' hospitality and friendliness.

The books almost never present Arabs of the middle class, professionals, or intellectuals. This is especially puzzling in view of the fact that the Arab professionals, citizens of the State of Israel, occupy a noticeable place in Israeli society, for example in hospitals as doctors or auxiliary personnel, or in schools in the role of teachers. Also, in the occupied territories, there is a considerable segment of intelligentsia, which does not appear in the books. Finally, the books relatively ignore the fact that, since 1979, Israel has had a peace treaty with Egypt. This dramatic event could have led to a better acquaintance with Egyptian society and culture.

From Generation to Generation

The negative stereotyping, which is still evident, and the delegitimization, which was common in earlier periods, are transmitted to the students from the first early years of their formal education in the elementary school up to their last classes of high school, when they are in advanced adolescence. This negative stereotyping is not surprising: the Jewish perception is founded on violent experiences with Arabs, adherence to their own Zionist goals, the insistence on relating only their own narrative, the concentration exclusively on their own challenges and needs, the focusing on Jews as victims, a lack of sensitivity and empathy to the aspirations of others, and the overall negation of the Arab case — all lead to the negative presentation of Arabs as such.

It was only in the late 1970s and 1980s that there first appeared books that provided an alternative presentation of the Arabs. Only the last few years of the 1990s saw the publication of history textbooks that can be seen as marking a new alternative trend that tries to present a more balanced and multidimensional presentation of the Arabs, in general, and of the Palestinians, in particular. But such books are few in number and limited in content. Their appearance is frequently accompanied by political outcry, media controversy, and political debate.

This review of the school textbooks suggests that, over the years, generations of Israeli Jews were taught a negative and often delegitimizing view of Arabs. The parents and the grandparents of the present generation were provided with the same negative image of the Arabs in their school textbooks as we see today, within the context of the prolonged Jewish-Arab conflict. One might add that it takes many years to rewrite school textbooks and a few generations to change the societal beliefs about the stereotyping and delegitimization of the Arabs.

References

Apple, M.W. (1979). *Ideology and Curriculum.* London: Routledge & Kegan Paul.

Bar-Gal, Y. (1993). *Moledet and Geography in Hundred Years of Zionist Education.* Tel Aviv: Am Oved (Hebrew).

—— (1994). "The Image of the 'Palestinian' in Geography Textbooks in Israel." *Journal of Geography* 93: 224–32.

Bar-Tal, D. (1998). "The Rocky Road towards Peace: Societal Beliefs Functional to Intractable Conflict in Israeli School Textbooks." *Journal of Peace Research* 35: 723–42.

Bar-Tal, D. & Zoltak, S. (1989). "Images of an Arab and Jewish-Arab Relations in School Readers." *Megamot,* 301–17 (Hebrew).

Bourdieu, P. (1973). "Cultural Reproduction and Social Reproduction." In R. Brown, ed., *Knowledge, Educational and Cultural Change.* London: Tavistock.

Brosh, H. (1997). "The Sociocultural Message of Language Textbooks: Arabic in the Israeli Setting." *Foreign Language Annals* 30:311–26.

Down, A. G. (1988). Preface in H. Tyson-Bernstein, *A Conspiracy of Good Intentions: America's Textbook Fiasco.* Washington, D.C.: The Council for Basic Education.

Eden, S. (1971). *On the New Curricula.* Jerusalem: Maalot (Hebrew).

Eisenstadt, S. N. (1967). *Israeli Society.* London: Weidenfeld and Nicholson.

Firer, R. (1985). *The Agents of Zionist Education.* Tel Aviv: Sifriyat Poyalim (Hebrew).

Luke, A. (1988). *Literacy, Textbooks, and Ideology.* London: Palmer Press.

Podeh, E. (2002). The Arab-Israeli Conflict in Israeli History Textbooks — 1948–2000. Westport, Conn.: Bergin & Garvey.

Zohar, N. (1972). *The Arab's Image in a Reader.* Master thesis submitted to the Hebrew University, Jerusalem (Hebrew).

CHAPTER SIXTEEN

THE POLITICIZATION OF PALESTINIAN CHILDREN
An Analysis of Nursery Rhymes

Nafez and Laila Nazzal

The process of political socialization of Palestinian children in the West Bank is a consequence of the war-like situation that has prevailed since 1967. It is rooted in a number of factors: direct contact with the Israeli occupational forces; the closure of kindergartens, schools, and universities; the media, especially the daily airing on television of confrontations between Palestinian youths and Israeli soldiers; the graffiti on walls used to communicate messages to the public; and conversations in homes and schools revolving around arrests, deportations, injuries, blowing up of homes, and the killing of neighbors or relatives.

Nursery schools in the West Bank have served as an institutional system that has reinforced this politicization of Palestinian children.

Teachers and peers have acted as significant socializing agents, instilling political norms through the teaching of rhymes from pamphlets, books, and tapes distributed by the Palestinian underground leadership. By constant repetition of a few stanzas over a period of two or three weeks, the children memorized them. Accompanying the rhymes, usually half-chanted, half-spoken, were gestures such as the victory sign, a clenched fist, a commando posture, the pointing to an imaginary flag, or the upright stance of a soldier marching in the underground popular army. Constant reiteration of the rhymes became part of the daily routine in schools. When a teacher had to leave the classroom for one reason or another, the tape recorder was left on, with a tape repeating the rhymes to the children.

The purpose of this study is to analyze the content of rhymes taught to three- to six-year-old Palestinian children in West Bank schools during the Intifada. The rhymes are categorized according to themes and type of school.

General Themes

Palestinian Patriotism

Pride in being Palestinian is fuelled by the resistance to the Israeli occupation of the territories since 1967, and particularly by the Intifada which began in 1987. Children grew up with stories and anecdotes of homes left behind, and of lush and fertile fields taken by the Israelis when the Palestinians were driven out of Palestine in 1948. The rhymes express a consistent, almost obsessive longing for a homeland and a flag that flutters in the sky. Everything is viewed from the perspective of fighting and acquiring a country and a homeland. In the rhymes, the homeland is idealized as free and liberated, where the Palestinians are reunited with their families.

My Homeland

My country, my country
How pretty it is
My family and my home

Under its sky
My country, my country,
We are its protectors
The land of plenty,
We are its liberators.
The flowers of the valley,
Their fragrance disseminates throughout the land.

Liberation through Rebellion

Because the land of Palestine was lost through wars, revolution as the only means to freedom and to regaining the lost land is another common theme. In the rhymes, those who struggle to regain their land would be blessed; thus, militarism becomes synonymous with heroism. Underlying the hope that victory is near is a challenge to the Israelis that, despite all that they do to the Palestinians, the latter will not give up and will eventually prevail. This gives purpose to their lives and helps them overcome their despair.

My Nation

I sang my song
In my country, on my holiday.
I am but a child,
But I have a mature mind...
With determination and precision,
I listed all the victories
I, in the love of my country
All my strength and struggle,
I see my country in my heart
A picture of greatness indeed.

Yearning for Freedom from Oppression

As a result of Israeli oppression, many Palestinians were incarcerated in Israeli jails. Even those who were not in prison suffered from the daily violations and infringements on human rights. In the following rhyme, a bird is envied because of its freedom, and it is extolled to inform the world of the oppression of the Palestinians who have lived under occupation for the past 27 years. The following rhyme is an ode under Israeli occupation and a catalogue of Israel's injustices:

I Envy You, O Bird

I envy you, O bird
You are free, unhampered
And I am an oppressed prisoner.

I envy you, O bird
Rescue me, O bird.

They took away my father in the middle of the night
And imprisoned him.
They humiliated him and beat him,
From his home they deported him...

My grandfather's house they destroyed,
And bulldozed it with its furniture
And my people, they scattered
From their lands, they exiled...

My brother stoned them and lighted a fire
To drive them away from the house,
To protect his younger brothers...

My sister is among the walls
Protecting the Aqsa with fire
To return the oppression of the cunning
With her brothers, the revolutionaries.

I envy you, O bird
Rescue me, O bird.

Go and tell, O bird

Inform all the houses.
Tell the people and all the birds.
What you saw of oppression,
Tell them, O bird.

Loss of Identity

Another theme which laments the Palestinian predicament of stateless-
ness revolves around the question of identity. The identity card that all
Palestinians must present at checkpoints or whenever they are stopped
by Israelis is symbolic of their loss of identity. The worst thing that could
happen to a person is to have his identity card confiscated by the Israelis. The identity cards achieved a particular significance during the
Intifada:

They stopped me at the border
And they asked for my identity card.
I told them it's in Jaffa
Hidden with my grandmother.
The words I said
Divided them into two groups
One group asking the "whys"
The other asking "where."

I cried, "Palestine"
They divided me into two halfs
One half on the border
The other half in my grandmother's lap
My grandmother, who is hiding
In a house I don't know where
My identity card put away, hidden in some place
They want to burn it
And to erase it from the world....

Rebellion and Resistance

The Palestinians attempted to resolve the pivotal matter of identity by portraying themselves as commandos or freedom fighters. The Intifada saw the emergence of new idealized characters, such as the vigilante-hero, who was often portrayed as the Robin Hood of the Palestinians. These vigilantes-heroes were masked teenagers who had taken upon themselves the task of harassing and executing collaborators, patrolling Palestinian roads and towns, extracting "taxes" from Palestinian industrialists, and collecting contributions from the masses to aid the needy Palestinians. The aspiration of young Palestinians in the Occupied Palestinian Territories (OPT) was to serve in this popular underground army:

> Papa bought me a gift,
> An automatic machine gun and rifle.
> When I grow up
> I'll enter the army of liberation.
> The army of liberation taught us
> How to liberate our homeland.

Palestinian Self-Reliance

At the outbreak of the Intifada, self-reliance, independence, and defiance, as well as steadfastness and determination, characterized the image of the new Palestinian.

Be Prepared

Be prepared
And be lions
And die martyrs
For the sake of the nation
Palestine is my land
My soul, my obligations
I sacrifice my child
For the liberation of my nation

Be prepared, be prepared
My country, my country
I am sounding the trumpet of war
I am prepared.

Strike Days

Strike days became the backbone of the Intifada. These were observed throughout the OPT and varied from a three-day period to honor a martyr, to a one-day general strike in protest against the establishment of a Jewish settlement in the West Bank.

Strike! Strike!
In Gaza and the West Bank
Strike! Strike!
Today, and tomorrow strike
We have legitimate demands
We want a homeland and freedom
Freedom through revolution
The revolution needs burning coals of fire...

The rain is coming, coming
It carries a tale and a narrative
It tells of children
Who ignite the revolution with stones.

It was the children of Palestine who instigated the revolution of stones, and the following rhyme pays homage to them. It also simultaneously threatens collaborators accused of working for Israel:

Stones here and stones there
The night goes and the day comes
The children are fearless in the face of the Israelis.
We do not fear
The tents of the desert [this is a reference to Ketziot prison
    in the Negev]

Nor the shooting of live ammunition
Nor the breaking of bones
Nor the demolition of homes
The United Command adopted a resolution
To eliminate the collaborators, the traitors and all evil
men.

Normalization of the Abnormal

Throughout the rhymes taught to West Bank children runs the theme that violent death is common and normal. Thus it became commonplace to expect and be proud of the fact that family members died for the liberation of the land. Blood and violence were explainable and justified in the struggle to regain one's country. They were part of the Palestinians' daily life, and martyrdom became an important dimension of the uprising. The *shahid*, or martyr, who died in the struggle against the Israelis was glorified and revered. The funeral was celebrated as a wedding, and instead of the customary tears and wailing, there were the ululations of happiness. The anniversary of the death was commemorated annually. Those who became handicapped, as so many did during the Intifada, were hailed as heroes. The handicap became a badge for having fought for the homeland. The rhyme that follows rationalizes death and simultaneously makes sense of it:

O mother, don't cry for me
I am leaving to fight,
Bring me those to whom I will bid farewell.
My tender mother encourage me.
I ask God to allow me to return.
My brothers and I are commandos.
I hear the cannon balls in the port,
Like the music of the *'ude* and the *kamanja*.
Revolution was created for the brave
And my ancestors were commandos.

Hatred of Jews

We also found rhymes expressing hatred of Jews. For a child whose house had been demolished, hatred and killing became revenge for the fact that he was now homeless, that his family's belongings were stacked in a couple of Red Cross tents. But underlying all this is fear of the Jews as represented by Israeli soldiers. Negative traits characterize the Jews who are seen as the victimizers, the culprits who stole Palestinian land and established their Jewish state on it.

The hatred is presented in blatant dehumanizing and derogatory terms. In some rhymes, they are referred to as "son of a dog" or "like a dog." References to animals is common in Arabic-Islamic culture, but it is pertinent to point out that there is a stratification in the animal kingdom. The dog is the lowest; the camel and the lion are the highest, because the former is noted for its utility among the Bedouins in the desert, and the latter for its ferociousness and courage:

> Palestine is our country
> The Jews our dogs
> Put one branch on top of another
> May Allah break the Jews,
> Put one bag on top of another bag
> May Allah release the prisoners
>
> PLO yes, Israel no
> Palestine yes!

Thematic Differences in the Rhymes

Since the outbreak of the Intifada in 1987, different political factions established nursery schools on the West Bank to promote and garner support for their ideology. Thematic differences in the contents of the rhymes reflected the particular ideology of the faction. For example, rhymes taught in nursery schools that identified with the Islamic trend emphasized liberation through Islam, the Prophet Muhammad's confrontation with the Jews in Medina, protection of Al-Aqsa Mosque and nostalgia for the victories of the Islamic past. The PLO national-ist rhymes make reference to religion, but quantitatively, there is more stress on Palestinian nationalism, love of the land, the role of women in the struggle, and commemoration of the date of establishment of the various factions.

A. Islamic Nursery Schools

The Revolution Must Be Islamic

The Islamist movements— Hamas, the Islamic Resistance Movement, the Muslim Brothers and Islamic Jihad — believe that Islam is the only unifying element for the people in the Middle East. States and leaders come and go and are constantly changing. Islam is the only means to achieving the solidarity and unity needed for the liberation of Palestine. Moreover, to be successful, the revolution must be led by an Islamic army.

My Country

Revolt, revolt and let the revolution be Islamic
Revolt, revolt and live free for eternity.

The rhymes taught to children in the religious schools claim that all of Palestine is an Islamic *Waqf.* Accordingly, all of Palestine, and not just the West Bank and Gaza Strip, should be liberated from the Jews and declared an Islamic state. The following illustrates this:

The West Bank, Gaza Strip,
Occupied territories
1967 plus 1948
Equals all of Palestine,
Our Islamic identity
From the river to the sea.

Protection of Al-Aqsa

Many of the rhymes also call for the protection of Al-Aqsa Mosque, a symbol of Islamic identity. The fighting of the Holy War (Jihad) to liberate all the holy places from the infidels is a prime objective in the rhymes of religious nursery schools:

The Jasmines

We are the buds of the jasmine
In the nursery of Muslims
With forgiveness, purity and solidarity
And in the morrow, we will creep as armies,
To challenge the occupiers
And if Al-Aqsa calls us
To reconquer it from the occupiers
We will reconquer what we have lost.

Nostalgia for Past Islamic History

Another theme taught by Islamic-supported nurseries is the nostalgic reference to historical Muslim heroes and famous battles. Not only were these important battles sung about, but they were also commemorated by the different Islamic factions that called for strikes on these days:

In the vicinity of Al-Aqsa, we sprouted
We, the bunches of lily
And with justice, we affirmed
We challenged
They led us to conquest once
Khalid, Sa'ad and Tareq.

A particular reference is made to Khaibar, a Jewish tribe that dwelled outside of Medina, whom Muhammad and his followers attacked, because they thought they were conspiring against them. The connotation was that the Muslims succeeded in defeating the Jews once, and they would repeat that victory:

Khaibar, Khaibar,
O Jews,
Muhammad's army
Will return.

B. NATIONALIST NURSERY SCHOOLS

Palestinian Patriotism

The rhymes taught at nursery schools supported by the different PLO political factions (PFLP, DFLP, and Fatah) deal with national and secular issues. The following rhyme reflects the love of land and identity, a major theme taught to Palestinian children:

They ask me who I am
I am a child of Palestine
They ask me, "Where do you live?"
I live in the land of my ancestors.
They ask me, "How can you live in humiliation and be patient?
Why not leave and emigrate to the West?"
I answer, "The countries of the West are not for me."
Palestine is my homeland
Home to all of my hopes.

The Role of Women in the Struggle

What stands out in the nationalist and secularist schools is the role of women fighting alongside men and doing their part to liberate the land from oppression:

Prepare my people,
The revolutionaries have emerged
Enough dispersion, enough exile
You will return

The sons of the nation are lined up to protect the land
Young men and women, teenagers and all.

Special events, such as Mothers' Day, which falls on March 21, were also politicized.

Mother's Day
Your holiday, O mother
The holiday of sacrifice,
Giving and persevering.

The holiday of meeting
My Palestinian mother of our land.
May every year be filled with
Thousands and thousands of blessings upon you.

Conclusion

Rhymes taught in West Bank nursery schools during the Intifada became a means of socializing the children politically, of raising their political consciousness, and ensuring the transmission of the political culture across generations. The learning of rhymes reinforced the children's ability to internalize such political issues as nationality, identity, and resistance to the Israeli occupation. To the children, these rhymes were not fictional or imaginative, but were valid and consistent with their everyday normal reality, and were reflective of their experiences and surroundings.

The rhymes also served as catharsis, a sort of release for the continued tension that the children witnessed. They attempted to make sense of the Palestinian children's world in order to alleviate the daily distress of their lives. They allowed them to come to terms with the political turmoil surrounding them and helped turn the abnormal situation into a normal and acceptable one. As blood and violent death became part of the children's lives, they had no qualms about reciting or chanting a rhyme about driving Jews from their land. Hatred and revenge were reactions to the fact that now they had no home, or that a parent or sibling limped, or was killed. The rhymes rationalized all this violence, explained the brutality, and gave purpose to their lives, helping them overcome their desperation under Israeli occupation.

Chapter Seventeen

Schoolbooks in the Making: From Conflict to Peace

A Critical Analysis of the New Palestinian Textbooks for Grades One and Six

Sami Adwan

Since the early 1950s, Palestinians have been using the Jordanian and Egyptian curricula and textbooks in West Bank and Gaza schools respectively. These texts were subjected to complete censorship by the Israeli military governor in charge of Palestinian education from 1967 until 1993. During this period, whole books were banned from schools; words and, sometimes, whole sections of textbooks were deleted. A special agreement was signed in 1996 between the Jordanian and the Palestinian ministries of education, whereby the Palestinians would continue using the same Jordanian texts in Palestinian schools until they are able and ready to produce their own. At the start of the school year

2000/2001 the Palestinian Ministry of Education completed twenty-nine textbooks (see index) for grades one and six only. The plan is to stagger the production of textbooks, taking two grades at a time, so that the transition and the introduction of the new texts will be done incrementally and smoothly, and pupils will be prepared for it.

Composing textbooks is not an easy task. The new curriculum had to be implemented under serious constraints, like closures of the Palestinian National Authority (PNA) territories by the Israeli army, lack of funds, a deadlocked peace process, and the renewed outbreak of violence since September 2000. The Palestinians are thus compelled to develop their own textbooks in the absence of a national constitution and in a situation that can at best be described as "unfavorable" and a future that can only be viewed as grim and uncertain.

Despite the signing of agreements, Israeli practices continue to impede the freedom of movement of Palestinians. Both pupils and teachers meet with difficulties in trying to reach their schools and in crossing checkpoints. The same applies to university students and staff, leading to the extension of regular semesters, delays in graduation, and cancellation of summer schools.

The al-Aqsa Intifada has led to a really critical situation. Children live in a constant state of terror as their homes are shelled by tanks and helicopter gunships, and their schools are attacked by soldiers and/or settlers. Rubber bullets, live ammunition, and tear gas bombs are shot at pupils while they're in class or in the schoolyard. The atrocities and violence they see around them or hear about, like the killing of a twelve-year-old boy in the arms of his father in early October 2000, or the shelling of a school for visually disabled children in al-Bireh, have traumatized them.

What I partially described above clearly shows that the ordinary Palestinian has so far not experienced the fruits of a peace agreement in his/her daily life. This point is important because it brings up the question: What do Palestinians teach their children in the newly produced textbooks for grades one and six, especially regarding the Israeli-Palestinian conflict?

This paper will attempt to provide some answers to this question. To this end, I have analyzed the new Palestinian textbooks—in total eighteen (nine for grade one and nine for grade six). They are Arabic language, religion (Muslim and Christian), history, geography, civics and national education. Some of the textbooks come in two parts, one for each semester. Textbooks of general sciences, mathematics, technology, and Arabic handwriting were surveyed but not analyzed, because nothing in them relates to the Palestinian-Israeli conflict/relationship. The total number of textbooks that were not analyzed is eleven (five for grade one and six for grade six).

In reading the findings of textbook analysis, the following factors have to be taken into account:

- The Palestinian-Israeli conflict has not been completely or satisfactorily resolved. This means that both parties are not yet on full peaceful terms. They are in a situation that can best be characterized as "between war and peace," although in recent months the former has taken precedence over the latter. Also, differences exist in the perception of peace between Israelis and Palestinians. For Palestinians, real peace means a complete end to the Israeli occupation, the establishment of an independent, sovereign Palestinian state on the 1967 occupied land, with East Jerusalem as its capital, as well as the full implementation of the right of return for Palestinian refugees and/or their compensation (UN Resolution 194). Israelis, on the other hand, perceive peace as a no-conflict/war situation and maintaining the status quo. Many Israelis think that peace agreements ended the conflict, while Palestinians think of them as a means to ending the conflict.

- Textbooks have to reflect the realities of a society—past, present, and future. If textbooks alienate children from their daily life, they will lose their legitimacy and the interest of the children. They cannot ignore the feelings, hopes, and aspirations of a society. In conflict situations, textbooks have always been used as a means of presenting the other side in a negative perspective or stereotyping; legitimizing the national ideology and de-legitimizing that of the other through indoctrination; and upholding the claim of "self" as always right and "they" as always wrong (Firer, 1999; Adwan, 1999). Thus, texts in conflict areas reflect the "war culture" and not the "peace culture." No one is to blame for this. It is worth noting that it took the Germans, Polish, and French more than ten years after the end of the Second World War to start looking at and modifying their textbooks. In the Palestinian-Israeli case, the conflict is still ongoing, even escalating. This presents the education authorities with real challenges and difficulties regarding what to write and how to write it, and what context and direction to take.

- Education and textbooks are not neutral or objective and never have been or should be. They include the legitimate knowledge of the peoples/states, even in the most decentralized systems of education. They are the means of relating to one's own culture, identity, and future.

- The analysis of textbooks cannot be done efficiently without a full understanding of the local language and culture. Language is not only a set of symbols that can be translated—it is actually the main cultural vehicle of any society, including its values, attitudes, humor, norms, customs, etc. Speaking a language that is not one's mother tongue does not fully qualify a person to analyze textbook contents, for textual analysis is not only an analysis of the explicit parts, but also includes the implicit parts as well. This often leads to misunderstandings on the part of non-native speakers.

- Palestinians have been living under foreign rule for so long that their identity is shattered, their culture is oppressed, and their economy is destroyed. They have been considered strangers in their own land. Their textbooks have to challenge this. They have to start building their national identity and ethos, relating to their culture and environment not as strangers. They have to teach their children their songs, customs, stories and, at the same time, entertain hopes for a better future.

The Textbooks—Perception of Self and Others

The new Palestinian textbooks describe Palestinians through various examples of daily activities. There is much emphasis on the way the Palestinians live in their cities, towns, and refugee camps, and on their culture and heritage. The general description of Palestinians as victims of the Zionist ideology and Israeli occupation is clearly seen in the texts. Palestinians are also described as religious people and texts portray the significant role religion plays in their daily life.

At the same time, Palestinian pupils learn to look positively at others. Negative stereotyping of Israelis or Jews is absent. Jews are even presented in a favorable light. This is clear in the story mentioned in the Islamic Education textbook for Grade Six, part I, pp. 82–83, which refers to an incident when Prophet Mohammad went out of Mecca and met a tribe and he asked them, "Are you affiliated with the tribe of the Jews?" They said, "Yes," and then he asked them, if so, "Can I meet with you?" They said, "Yes." Then they met, the text adds. This means, had they not been affiliated with the Jewish tribes, he (the Prophet) would not have met them. The same text mentions, "The Jews in the Peninsula have foreseen that Prophet Mohammad would come soon, and they even waited for his birth" (pp. 83–84). Similarly, in Islamic Education (for Grade Six, part II, p. x), the Prophet Moses and other Jewish prophets are presented in very positive ways. The pupils are asked to respect "the heavenly religions" (*Civic Education* for Grade Six, p. 68).

The History of Arabs and Muslims (Grade Six, p. 20) discusses the spread of Judaism before Islam in Yathrib (al-Madinah), Khaibar, and Yemen. The text adds (p. 24) that both Muslims and Jews respected the agreements and the conventions that they signed between themselves, and encourages pupils "to respect the People of the Book [Jews and Christians], their properties and religious ceremonies" (p. 25).

Examples of assignments include the following: "Name religions that existed in the Peninsula before Islam" (*The History of Arabs and Muslims*, Grade Six, p. 22), or "What is the position of Islam toward other believers and the followers of the heavenly religions?" and the pupils are asked to relate cases or situations in Islamic history that focus on tolerance and compassion for others (*National Education*, Grade Six, p. 72). The same chapter warns pupils of the danger to societies of extremism and fanaticism (p. 64). Pupils are asked "to write a paper on evidence from the Holy Books (the Koran, the New Testament, and the Old Testament) that call for tolerance and the rejection of extremism" (*National Education*, Grade Six, p. 65). "Pupils are also enjoined to visit holy sites of all religions." Chapter 3 in the textbook (pp. 64–82) discusses such human values as justice, freedom, equality, honesty, and the search for peace.

Tolerance, Peace and Pacifism

The Christian religious textbook (for Grade One, p. 15) stresses tolerance and emphasizes the values of peace on earth and happiness for all people (p. 33). Tolerance between Christians and Muslims in Palestinian society is widely brought out in a discussion of Palestinian society in the *National Education* textbook (Grade Six, pp. 12–14) which states that "Palestinian society is characterized by tolerance and brotherhood between Christians and Muslims" (p. 13) and pupils are requested "to implement this in their daily practice." The text further asks the pupils to collect photos of Islamic and Christian holy sites and to place them on a chart (practical assignment, p. 14). An example of a peace-oriented assignment is the following: "Olive trees are the symbol of peace, please discuss this in the context of the Palestinian situation now" (*Our Beautiful Language*, Grade Six, part I, p. 82).

One of the educational goals mentioned in chapter 1 of *The Principles of Human Geography* (Grade Six, p. 3) is that "pupils are encouraged to uphold good relations with neighboring countries." The same text (pp. 41–42) explains to pupils that "killing men is a heinous act and is an outcome of wars," in an attempt to warn pupils of the devastating effects of wars and conflicts. The text goes further and promotes tolerance and coexistence, supports democracy and justice, the respect of diversity, and the freedom of expression. Pupils are encouraged in the use of peaceful means in resolving disputes and disagreements and in shunning extremism. Negotiations, dialogue, and passive resistance are promoted (*National Education* for Grade Six, pp. 64–78), and pupils are asked to role-play how to peacefully resolve a problem or a conflict (p. 78).

Our *Beautiful Language* textbook for Grade Six (part II, pp. 104–110) devotes a chapter to Ghandi and his pacifist approach to liberation. Pupils are expected to "talk about passive resistance" (p. 104) and "to give examples of non-violent resistance of the Palestinian Intifada of 1987" (pp. 108, 114). Pupils are asked "to collect some photos of Palestinian non-violent methods in the 1987 Intifada," and to illustrate such methods by writing a short biography of figures like Nelson Mandela" (p. 114). Dialogue and negotiation as means of learning and dealing with the Other are emphasized to a great degree in the National Education textbook (Grade One, pp. 14–21); pupils are encouraged to "love and not to hate" (*Our Beautiful Language*, Grade Six, part II, p. 111).

Jihad (Holy War) and Its Ethics

What does Jihad really mean? To fully comprehend the concept, I read the Holy Koran and *al-Hadeeth* (Prophet Mohammad's words and acts), as well as reference books that discuss Jihad, like the comprehensive *Fiqh al-Sunnah* by al-Sayed Sabiq (1980). Jihad is a holy war, but it is not an act of aggression (Sabiq, 1980). In fact, it is a defensive war in which Muslims are ordered to participate in accordance with certain conditions or stipulations: if they are attacked, or if they are stripped of their land and property. Muslims are also requested to fight oppression and injustice and to defend Islam. This is very explicitly mentioned in Surat al-Hujorat: Ayat 15 in the Holy Koran (*Islamic Education*, Grade Six, part I, p. 12). Muslims are to fight to defend the freedom of worship for all people: Jews, Christians, and Muslims. In Islam only a defensive war is a legitimate war (Azzam, pp. 103–104).

Pupils are encouraged to love and defend their country, an act that in Islam becomes a religious duty. This can be done by taking care of the land, the environment, the people, and by cooperating with others on the basis of equality, justice, and mutual respect (*Islamic Education*,

Grade Six, part 1, p. 68). Jihad thus entails undergoing hardships in various areas in life, like studying, working, traveling, and being away from one's family. Of course, Jihad also means people are to defend themselves when they are attacked, but in the process they have to be humane and not to commit any war crimes or dehumanize others, nor should Muslims fight for monetary gain or fame (Azzam, 1975, pp. 102–111, and Sabiq, 1980, pp. 5–64).

Muslims are thus allowed to fight only to defend themselves and should first exhaust all peaceful means to resolve a conflict. Fighting then is not a Muslim's first option, and if the opponent stops the fighting and calls for peace, a Muslim will have to heed the call and end the fighting. Clearly, a misunderstanding of Jihad has arisen among certain parties, whereby Jihad is misconstrued as a belligerent and violent act. As mentioned earlier, therein lies the danger of textbook analysis without a full comprehension and knowledge of the indigenous language and culture.

Martyrdom

Every nation bears great respect for its leaders and legendary figures, especially those who have paid with their lives to preserve and defend their national identity. They are the heroes of the people and become part of their culture and collective narrative. The Jewish people refer to the "pioneers," to members of the Haganah, Etzel, and Irgun, as their heroes (Firer, 1999/2000). Palestinians look at *al-mujahideen* (freedom fighters) and the *fidayeens* (those who sacrifice their lives for the sake of their land and people) as their heroes. In both Israeli and Palestinian textbooks, the heroes of the other side are considered monsters, terrorists, and the "bad guys" (Firer, 1999/2000; Adwan, 2001). This is how the other side, in general, and the heroes/leaders, in particular, are presented in times of conflict/war, not only in school textbooks, but also in other ways of socialization, like the media, popular stories, drawings, cartoons, graffiti, etc. The image of the enemy/other is always distorted in a culture of war.

Clearly, the general orientation of Palestinian textbooks is to have pupils respect martyrs and to hold them in high regard. The notion of martyrdom is greatly valued in Palestinian society. Examples can be found throughout the textbooks: Those who are killed fighting oppression and sacrifice their lives defending Islam, their people and land are considered martyrs. Pupils are thus asked to learn about martyrs, who they are, what they did throughout Arab history. They are asked, for example, to "write a letter about the feelings of a martyr's mother" (*Our Beautiful Language*, Grade Six, p. 58). This theme is echoed in a poem by the Palestinian poet Abdel Latif Aqel, entitled "The Poem of the Intifada," which deals with martyrs and their mothers (p. 130). A black-and-white photo of Izzeddine al-Qassam, who became a martyr in 1935 while fighting the British, is also included as a way of showing respect to martyrs (*National Education*, Grade Six, p. 15).

Jerusalem

The city of Jerusalem is considered holy by all parties involved in the Palestinian-Israeli conflict. In all Palestinian textbooks where Jerusalem (al-Quds al-Sharif) is mentioned, reference is specifically made to Arab East Jerusalem that was occupied by Israel in the 1967 war. This is a fact clearly stated in all UN resolutions. Israel, in violation of all international agreements and conventions (the Fourth Geneva Convention and UN Security Council resolutions 242 and 338), unilaterally annexed East Jerusalem in 1980. All Israeli texts, on the other hand, refer to the city as "Israel's united capital" in a clear denial of its status as an occupied city, as well as the denial of the Palestinians' rights in the city (Firer, 1999/2000).

Naturally, the importance of East Jerusalem to Palestinians (Muslims and Christians) is stressed in the textbooks. Its holiness for all religions is brought out. Pictures of Christian and Muslim holy places are included in many textbooks. Pictures of the Dome of the Rock, al-Aqsa Mosque, and the Holy Sepulcher are used to symbolize Jerusalem. The Western Wall is also called the al-Buraq Wall where the Prophet Mohammad tied his horse on his nightly journey to Heaven from Mecca. In the texts, East Jerusalem is also presented as the political capital of the future Palestinian state (*National Education*, Grade Six, p. 29). The importance of Jerusalem to Palestinians is not only religious or political; Jerusalem has always been the economic, cultural, educational, and health center for Palestinians since the division of the city in 1948. It is basically a symbol of their national identity (Adwan, 2001).

Maps in Textbooks

The Palestinian-Israeli conflict is often characterized as a protracted conflict, still far from being settled. This situation spills over into the treatment of maps. In the new Palestinian textbooks, the borders of the independent Palestinian state are supposed to be based on what was stated in the November 15, 1988, Declaration of Independence, i.e., UN resolutions since 1947 (*National Education* for Grade Six, p. 32). However, borders have not been settled yet in peace talks between Israelis and Palestinians. The delineation of maps thus poses a problem. Some maps included in Palestinian textbooks, for example, the *National Education* (Grade Six, p. 42) point to the boundaries of the Palestinian national territories as those of 1967. Other maps refer to the Jewish settlements in the West Bank and the Gaza Strip within the clearly delineated lines of the 1967 occupied territories (p. 15). In one exercise, pupils are asked to look at a map and indicate the telephone area code numbers of all the Palestinian districts (*Our Beautiful Language*, part II, Grade Six, p. 27).

It should be noted that despite its long history of producing textbooks (since 1925), Israel still does not distinguish the Palestinian areas in its school textbooks, or even mention the Palestinians by name, except for the writings of the new historians and some textbooks, especially by Daniel Bar-Tal or Eyal Naveh, but almost never in other school textbooks.

In her report on Israeli textbooks, Dr. Ruth Firer from the Truman Institute for the Advancement of Peace states that "there is no mention of Palestinian towns or cities at all in Israeli textbooks, and, whenever they are mentioned, they are very few compared to Israeli towns and cities" (Firer, 1999/2000). The occupied territories of Palestine are still called Judea and Samaria (their biblical names, a terminology used by right-wingers) and all of Jerusalem is depicted and referred to as one united city. The borders of Israel run from the Mediterranean Sea (west) to the River Jordan (east), without any indication of the occupied territories. Only the names of the Jewish settlements in the occupied territories are mentioned. The few Palestinian cities when mentioned are referred to in their Hebraicized names, like "Shchem" for "Nablus" (ibid).

Admittedly, the subject of maps is a sensitive issue and should be tackled only after all borders and lines between the future independent State of Palestine and the State of Israel are demarcated within the context of negotiations between the two sides. Any criticism of maps in either texts or atlases before this materializes is premature, unreasonable, and unfair.

The Love for Palestine

The new Palestinian textbooks address Palestinian life. They talk about the Palestinian homeland, culture, values and norms, economics, politics, history, religions, and their suffering as a result of the Israeli occupation. They also talk about the Palestinians' dreams of their homeland: "Palestine Is Green." Discuss a farmer's family, the orange and the lemon groves, and the water in Palestine is an example of a topic for an essay (*Our Beautiful Language*, Grade One, part I, pp. 71–102). Emphasis is clearly placed on the Palestinians' identity when they are asked to state "who they are," and "from where they come" and "what their nationality is" (*National Education*, Grade One, part I, pp. 8–10). Pupils are called to take care of Palestine by defending it, keeping it clean and beautiful, farming its land, and cooperating with each other (*Islamic Education*, Grade Six, part I, p. 68).

"My Home Is Palestine" is a full lesson where students are expected to know the geography and civilization of Palestine. The lesson includes natural scenery, and pictures of ancient religious locations (*National Text*, Grade One, part II, pp. 47–52). Stress is placed on the land of grandparents in order to maintain Palestinian identity, heritage, and the sense of belonging (p. 58). As an assignment, pupils are asked to "discuss with each other the importance of agriculture in Palestine" and to "ask their grandmothers and grandfathers and write a report about the kind of agriculture they used 50 years ago, the farming tools, the time of harvesting and to compare it with those of today" (*The Principles of Demographic Geography*, Grade Six, p. 69).

Dispossession, dispersion, and life in the diaspora have characterized Palestinian society throughout its history. In the textbooks, a refugee camp is not considered the original place of residence of the Palestinians, but a "temporary place [I] am forced to live in, and all Palestinians wait for the moment that each Palestinian would be able to return to his/her city or town from which s/he was forced to flee." This is what the *Islamic Education* textbook wants the pupils to understand from one of the lessons (Grade Six, part I, p. 69).

Our Beautiful Language (Grade Six, part I) is full of examples drawn from Palestinian life: homes, daily practices, the various professions, photographs of holy as well as ancient sites, trees (mostly olive, the symbol of peace in Palestine), the sources of stones for buildings, the refugee issue, and stories that emphasize Palestinian identity and culture (pp. 27, 31, 39, 45, 47, 58–59, 64–65, 72, 76–77, 82, 87, 93, 99, 107, 110, 115, 120–121, 123, 130, 141, and 163). Also part II for the same grade includes other examples of Palestinian life and heritage (pp. 17–18, 26, 31, 33, 40, 47, 61, 64, 75, 89–90, 103, 106, 110, 111, 114–115, and 131).

The *Civic Education* textbook for Grade One focuses mainly on developing the pupils' personal and national identities. Photos of Palestinian passports as well as birth certificates are included as signs of identity. Pupils are to learn their duties, their rights, and what constitutes good behavior. The *Civic Education* textbook for Grade Six focuses on how pupils should relate to their environment—natural and social. They also learn about cooperation with others, democracy as a concept and practice, non-governmental work, unions, societies, and how to fight crime and uphold teamwork.

Unit two of *National Education*, Grade Six, focuses on Palestinian national organizations (pp. 20–22), the PLO (pp. 22–25), the Palestinian National Council (pp. 26–28), the state (pp. 29–32), the constitution (pp. 33–35), the three authorities (pp. 36–40), the ministries (p. 40) administrative organizations (pp. 42–44), the judiciary and courts in Palestine (pp. 45–48), economic organizations, banks, factories, companies (pp. 48–56), societal organizations (pp. 56–60), and health organizations (pp. 60–63). The aim is to develop the pupils' understanding of their society, its structure, and their role in building their identity and ethos.

Unit three, "I and the Others" (pp. 64–82), includes and stresses the values of tolerance, freedom, justice, and equality, to teach pupils how to behave, how to treat others, and to encourage them to be productive and hardworking.

The textbooks, on the other hand, talk about Jewish settlements and their negative effects on Palestinians. Pupils are asked to "think how to face this" (*Islamic Education*, Grade Six, part I, p. 68). In the lesson on pollution, pupils are asked to "write a short report on the effect of settlements in polluting the environment" (*Demographic Geography*, Grade Six, p. 94), or "write a short report on the negative results of building Jewish settlements on Palestinian land" (*National Education*, Grade Six, pp. 18–19).

Palestinian National Identity

The textbooks of any nation should be able to reflect the life of its people—their collective narrative and memories. Pupils have the right to read about their history, their culture, their pain and suffering, their joys and happiness. Otherwise, textbooks become irrelevant and alien to pupils who will consequently lose all interest in them.

In the past, Palestinians had to use textbooks (Jordanian and Egyptian) that did not relate to them or to their culture or social and political aspirations. Presenting the reality of Palestinian life at this juncture in history is not an easy task. As mentioned earlier, the situation between Palestinians and Israelis is described as "between conflict and peace" or "on the road to peace." While the intention is to focus on peace and coexistence, the daily life of Palestinians is still characterized by suffering, closure and siege, house demolitions, land confiscation, and now by shelling and bombing.

It is very problematic to write textbooks in this paradoxical situation. How can Palestinians teach their children to love Israelis, when the only things they see and experience (from Israelis) are death, injuries, restrictions on movement, the destruction of their homes, the razing of their land and uprooting of trees, and starvation. For Palestinian children, Israelis are, so far, seen only as soldiers, settlers, and bulldozer operators.

I asked pupils from Grade Eight to express their perception of the present situation between Israelis and Palestinians through drawings. About 98 percent of the drawings depicted the killing and maiming of Palestinians, the shelling of their homes by tanks, helicopters, and heavy machine guns, the destruction and blocking of their roads, and the uprooting of their trees. Children cannot be duped into believing or learning the opposite of what they see and experience. It is too much and too soon to request the Palestinians to produce textbooks so far removed from reality. Love cannot be imposed on people; it has to blossom from within. Palestinians need justifications to perceive Israelis in a more positive light. This doesn't mean the Palestinians do not want to teach love and peace, but peace has to become a concrete reality.

In *National Education* (Grade Six, p. 70), a picture shows two clerics shaking hands—a Muslim and a Christian—to symbolize tolerance. The question arises: "Why is there is no Jewish religious figure with them?" In my opinion, it is a legitimate question, but, at the same time, such a scene is rather untimely. Palestinians still perceive Israelis as the main cause of their suffering. The inclusion of a rabbi in the picture is too premature to be accepted and envisioned by Palestinian pupils and society at large. The pupils will react to it with pain and with suspicion, since it is not their reality.

The situation on the ground has to improve dramatically and the relationship between Israelis and Palestinians has to move away from victimhood (victimizers/victims) (Dan Bar-On, 1999), for far-reaching changes to be accepted. To try to change people's thoughts and feelings without changing the reality is a form of patronization, and it, too, can be perceived as a form of oppression and manipulation.

Signing peace agreements is not enough to change attitudes and values between old foes, but they are necessary to start the process. Peace building needs grassroots work and time and space for people to mourn and heal. I fully agree with the first part of John F. Kennedy's famous statement, "Peace does not lie in charters and conventions alone. It lies in the hearts and minds of people." But, I would add that, for peace to grow in the hearts and minds of people, they first need to feel and live their humanity as free men, to be able to discover themselves, to decide for themselves, to regain their self-respect, and to restore their shattered identity.

Bibliography

A. Analyzed textbooks:

Abu-Khashan, Abdel Karim, et al. (2000). *Our Beautiful Language*, parts I & II, Grade Six. Attalah, Hanna, Father, et al. (2000). *Christian Religious Education*, Grade Six.

Attalah, Mahmoud, et al. (2000). *The Principles of Demographic Geography*, Grade Six.

—— (2000). *The History of Arabs and Muslims*, Grade Six.

Doufish, Khalil, et al. (2000). *National Education*, parts I & II, Grade One.

EI-Arouri, Farid, et al. (2000). *Civic Education*, parts I & II, Grade Six.

EI-Hayek, Nazih, Father, et al. (2000).*Christian Religious Education*, Grade One.

Kamal, Zahira, et al. (2000). *Civic Education*, parts I & II, Grade One.

Musalam, Omar, et al. (2000). *Our Beautiful Language*, parts I & II, Grade One.

Mustafa, T. Harnzah, et al. (2000). *Islamic Education*, parts I & II, Grade Six.

Shakarnah, A. Abdallah, et al. (2000). *Islamic Education*, parts I & II, Grade One.

B. Textbooks surveyed but not analyzed:

Abu-Khashan, Abdel Karim (2000). *Arabic Handwriting*, Grade Six.

Hamad, Ali Khalil, et al. (2000). *Mathematics*, parts I & II, Grade One.

Mass'ad, Fateen, et al. (2000). *Mathematics*, parts I & II, Grade Six.

Musalam, Omar, et al. (2000). *Arabic Handwriting*, Grade One.

Sa'ad, Mahmoud Hani, et al. (2000). *General Science*, parts I & II, Grade One.

Saia'rah, Ahmad, et al. (2000). *Technology*, Grade Six.

Sharia, Ziad Mustafa, et al. (2000). *General Science*, parts I & II, Grade Six.

3. General references:

Azzam, Abdel Rahman (1975). *The Eternal Message*: A Textbook for Grade Twelve. The West Bank Administration: The Office of Education.

Adwan, Sami (2001). *The Status of Jerusalem in Palestinian Texts*. Jerusalem: The Palestinian Consultancy Group (in press).

———— (1999/2000). "Analysis of the Palestinian Narrative of the Israeli/Palestinian Conflict in Palestinian History and Civic Education Texts: The Palestinian Refugee Problem and the 1967 War." Braunschweig, Germany: Georg Eckert Institut.

Bar-On, Dan, and Sami Adwan (1999). *The Role of Palestinian and Israeli NGOs in Peace Building*. Beit Jala: PRIME.

Firer, Ruth (1999/2000). "Analysis of the Israeli Narrative of the Israeli/Palestinian Conflict in Israeli History and Civic Education Texts: The Palestinian Refugee Problem and the 1967 War." Braunschweig, Germany: Georg Eckert Institut.

The Holy Koran.

Sabiq, al-Sayed (1980). *Fiqeh al-Sunnah* (Arabic), part III. Beirut: Dar al-Fiker.

This is a shorter version of a paper published in the fall of 2001 as part of a comprehensive study by Georg Eckert Institut, Braunschweig, Gennany.

CHAPTER EIGHTEEN

ISLAM AND DEMOCRACY
Are They Compatible?

Abdelmajid Charfi

Ever since September 11, 2001, the question of the connections between Islam and democracy, between Islam and terrorism and, more generally, violence has been very much on the agenda. In the booming colonial literature of a century ago, it was another question that was more frequently posed: that of the responsibility of Islam in the backwardness of the Muslim people, especially since it promotes fatalism and is allegedly opposed to freedom of choice and the spirit of initiative. We should ask ourselves whether these questions—or rather accusations—are pertinent, and whether Islam as a religion is effectively at the source of the obvious lack of democracy in many Muslim countries and, particularly, in the Arab world.

To start with, it should be pointed out, as an example, that Latin America has long suffered under dictatorial regimes run by corrupt military juntas and nobody, at least in the West, has thought of holding Christianity, the majority religion of the Latin American people, responsible for these dictatorships. Neither has anyone judged that the Orthodox religion of the Russians—who had allowed Communism to take root in their countries—was to blame for their unrelenting autocratic rule over the peoples of the defunct Soviet Union.

Why then this essentialist view of Islam which, supposedly, is incapable of evolution or change? And why also overlook the fact that the majority of Muslims are living today in Indonesia, Bangladesh, Malaysia, India, and elsewhere under democratic regimes—within the limits permitted by their socioeconomic conditions.

Fueled by Islamist Literature

It is true that a whole body of Islamist literature exists that is financed and encouraged in part by the Islam of petrol which feeds this essentialist view of Islam. It provides it with irrefutable arguments concerning the predilection of a fringe of Muslims for a caliphate regime and political systems that fall far short of the criteria for democracy. However, the general tendency is to take such a view at face value and to regard it as representative of a prevalent Muslim attitude, instead of placing it within its proper context. It is equally true that, throughout history, political power in the countries of Islam did not usually allow for citizen participation in civic affairs. But which power in pre-modern history was democratic in the sense that we understand it today?

This negative perception of Islam is without doubt being fueled by ideological rather than religious motives. It manifestly provides its detractors with a clean conscience to implement their policies of hegemony and exploitation under the guise of the struggle of good against evil, and the propagation of democracy, liberty, and human rights. They overlook the discrepancy posed by such justification with their selfish economic and strategic interests, and with their arrogant and criminal conduct, even according to international law and the basic principles of ethics. Nevertheless, although it is material interests which guide the politics of the big powers, neither the cultural nor the psychological dimensions are to be disregarded. In certain instances, they can be very important, albeit never determining. They serve rather to justify hegemonic and belligerent machinations, and to give a semblance of legitimacy for actions that are devoid of it.

A Degree of Nostalgia

Even if today's West has ceased to be the Christianity of the Middle Ages and is now largely secularized, its attitude towards the Muslim world remains tinged with the animosity and strife that have marked the shared history of both Muslims and Christians around the Mediterranean since the inception of Islam. The former remember with nostalgia the period when they were masters of Spain, the south of France and Sicily. The latter do not forget that countries which once were the cradle and centers of Christianity—Palestine in the first place, but also Syria, Egypt, Turkey, with towns charged with history and Christian symbols like Jerusalem, Antioch, Alexandria or Constantinople—have fallen under the rule of Islam. The religion of Christ has forever been banished from these lands, while its followers have dwindled to a minority.

It is not then by chance that the West, traditionally anti-Semitic, has installed Israel in the heart of the Arab world.[1] It was one way for the West to rid itself of the Jews; at the same time it was able to throw a western bridgehead in a part of the world it often perceived as basically hostile. And it is not the least paradoxical to see the traditionally anti-Jewish religious extreme right and ultra-conservatives—currently in the ascendance in the U.S.A.—give their unstinting support to the Zionist entity, as they believe this would hasten the Second Coming of Christ. In such a unique situation, not one leader has seen fit to decry the blatant denial of justice of which the Palestinians are victim, or the alleged Israeli democracy which treats the latter as second class citizens and practices a segregationist policy based on religion and race.

Why then does the West give such an importance to the establishment of democracy in Muslim countries? Everybody is familiar with the scores of analyses asserting that democracy is the best defense against the terrorism carried out by certain Islamist groups, operating almost everywhere around the world and striking blindly against innocent victims. These analyses can be accepted without reservation, provided Islam is not associated with such terrorist acts, even if their perpetrators insist on the fact.

In the name of Christian values, some militants of the pro-life movement in the U.S.A. have attacked doctors and clinics that practice abor-
tions. The Irish Catholics have perpetrated several terrorist acts against
their Protestant enemies. It does not mean that Christianity, which has
been abusively invoked in these cases, should be held responsible for
the reprehensible acts one commits in its name. Similarly, ultra-Orthodox Jewish settlers and Israeli soldiers armed to the teeth kill with
impunity peaceful citizens of the occupied territories, expel others from
their homes, blow up their houses, uproot their millenary trees, and destroy their crops under the false pretense of the fight against terrorism
and their religious right over the land of Palestine. It would be wrong,
however, to see in Judaism a religious or systematic hatred towards non-
Jews. The same measure should apply to Islam.

Understanding the Historical Context

One must always seek to understand the historical conditions which
lead to the reading of sacred texts in one way rather than in another.
It is in the nature of sacred texts to be susceptible to divergent, even
contradictory, interpretations, arising from a specific context, from the
expectations of the readers, or from the underlying cultural framework.
It is not possible then to assert that Islam is for or against democracy, or
for the equality of the sexes, freedom of conscience or any other value.
The mainstream readings, called orthodox, are in effect nothing but the
reflection of the preoccupation of the faithful during a certain period.
They may change; the faithful, however, need not recognize the changes.
This is completely justified, to the extent that the Prophetic messages
are systematically perverted under the influence of socio-historical factors, and because religion, in getting institutionalized, is transformed
into a congealed and dogmatic system of beliefs and non-beliefs. The
believers are then called upon to cut across successive layers of historical
interpretations in order to arrive at the original meaning of the founding texts.

 If militant Islamism, which is essentially political and is responsible
for a number of contemporary terrorist acts in and outside Muslim
countries, claims its action springs from a reading of the Qur'an and

the Prophetic Tradition which it considers as the only valid sources, it is because religious teaching in the majority of the traditional religious centers is far behind the modern advances grounded in the scientific achievements of the past two centuries. The Catholic Church had held anti-modernist attitudes until the Vatican II Council. The Muslims do not dispose of a clergy like that of Catholicism. With a historical retard in the religious domain as indeed in other domains, it is normal that we should witness among them all sorts of religiosities, each trying in its way to be faithful to the teachings of Islam. We are, in effect, in the presence of a manipulative process which profits those who have the means to influence public opinions through television satellites and other media that spout all day long a discourse both reactionary and retrograde.

Sunni Islam—which is in the majority—has always held a legitimistic position vis-à-vis the established powers. The Muslim clerics were ready to recognize any regime, even despotic, provided it conceded to them the monopoly of social control through the prerogatives of religious law which they are supposed to apply. Today, this position has become anachronistic by the fact that religious law is essentially universal, whereas the Muslims live in countries where the law is by nature territorial. The modern Muslim nation-states follow then a law where the reference to the *shari'a* is most tenuous if not totally absent, except in what relates to personal status, which remains in most cases subject to the rules of classical jurisprudence.

Not Unlike Other Religions

In other words, Islam is not free from the manipulation by the religious for social ends. All the traditional and pre-modern societies have experienced the system of laws justified by religion, which was considered the ultimate authority for the legitimization of the established order, including the political. Today, the aspirations of Muslims for democracy and the participation of citizens in the public sphere do not differ from the aspirations of other people, irrespective of creed, language, or color. The maintaining of undemocratic regimes, or frankly anti-democratic ones, that claim more or less openly a religious legitimacy, should be explained only by the fact that Muslim societies have not yet generally succeeded in modernizing their production and social systems, or in acquiring institutions that guarantee popular sovereignty. Agriculture, breeding, handicrafts, and small businesses are the most widespread means of production. Income from petrol is enough to cater to the needs of the population in certain countries. But almost in all Muslim countries, industrialization is either insufficient or simply inexistent. This shapes, directly and indirectly, the social configurations of the countries, not to mention that it is a necessary condition, albeit not sufficient, for the establishment of a democratic system.

Consequently, dealing with the question of democracy in terms of its compatibility or incompatibility with Islam is not a valid approach. Like all religions, Islam adapts to any political regime. This does not mean that all regimes are comparable in measuring up to its principles, far from it. To the contrary, our reading of the Muhammedian message leads to the assertion that in dispensing with intermediaries between man and the Divine, and ending the dependence of man on supernatural powers, human beings are enabled to fully exercise their freedom and responsibility. And what better system than democracy through which to exercise these two fundamentals? Consequently, any position at variance with this is nothing but a hangover from the past, doomed sooner or later to disappear or to be marginalized.

Those who seek to label Islam as a violent or despotic religion are on the wrong track. They would better be advised to address the origin of injustices and frustrations experienced by Muslims and to help in the emergence or the consolidation of conditions that promote the establishment of democracy, instead of pretending to impose it by the force of arms. They should also start by practicing democracy in their own international relations and the functioning of such institutions as the World Bank, the International Monetary Fund (IMF), or the UN Security Council. And finally, they could show their serious concern for democracy by ending their support, especially by covert means, in the Muslim world and elsewhere, for dictatorial regimes, since these tend to facilitate the exploitation, by foreign powers, of the riches of their own people.

Notes

1. "The hunting of Jews has always been a European sport. Now, the Palestinians, who had never practiced it, are paying the price," Eduardo Galeano, *Le Monde diplomatique*, August 2005, p. 10.

CHAPTER NINETEEN

ON OVERCOMING
ANTI-SEMITISM
AND ISLAMOPHOBIA

Yehuda Stolov

In this article I intend to discuss ways of overcoming Arab anti-Semitism and Israeli Arab-phobia and Islamophobia. I believe that my comments are relevant for a large variety of conflict contexts. My experience and knowledge come from the Middle East, from the Holy Land, and I will focus on this part of the world.

The nature of this experience leads to a second point. This article is based on many years of practical experience in using the approach it portrays, in active work for the building of human peace (between human beings and not just leaderships and politicians) in the Holy Land and the Middle East through interactive interfaith dialogue, mainly in the framework of the Interfaith Encounter Association (IEA) (www. interfaith-encounter.org). The ideas in it were not developed in an abstract way, as theoretical concepts, but as an ideological infrastructure

ave supplied the basis for IEA activities and are con-
igh intensive field testing in hundreds of events with
e. The ideas are supported by concrete successes on

point of introduction is also derived from the nature of
my experience. Prejudices and fears, mistrust and even hatred exist between Jews and Arabs, or as we prefer to look at them: between Jews,
Muslims, Christians, and Druze. Yet regardless of other factors that are
probably very important when analyzing these phenomena, the main
factor that makes it possible for these negative attitudes to prevail is
ignorance—both in the sense of knowing very little, if at all, about the
"other" and in the sense of ignoring the "other." Consequently, getting
to know each other in a deep and positive manner is the way to prevent
the possibility of these phenomena. My main focus—in my work, in my
life, and in this article—is on how this can be done in a most effective
way, through interactive interfaith encounter.

Finally, an introductory word about religion: the human desire for
better connection with the Divine (or whatever one chooses to call this
super-reality, which is beyond words anyway) and for meaning in and of
life is a very powerful force. The different paths in this quest are organized in what we call religions, which makes religions a very powerful
force with an ability to influence humans and to mobilize them to make
and take more out of themselves and go beyond where they would otherwise go. Being a very powerful force by itself does not make religion
good or bad. Like the less powerful forces, it can be both used and misused. What makes the difference between the two is the human who
works with the force—as the Jewish sages of the Talmud say: "If he is
worthy, the Torah becomes for him a drug of life; if he is not, it becomes
for him a drug of death."

How Do We Overcome Prejudices and Fears?

So how do we make sure that religion is for us, and others, "a drug of
life"? And how do we overcome the prejudices, fears, and even hatreds,
and replace them with respect, trust, and even friendship? It is beyond
the scope of this article to describe in detail that, at least for the Abra-

hamic religions, the second question is really part of the first. I will just say that, as all of these religions claim to lead humanity in its quest to God, it is clear that religious leaders have to overcome prejudices and fears and to build respect and trust in order for their leadership to be effective. For me, the answer to both questions is by being engaged in intensive interfaith encounter.

But who says that this answer is the correct one? Experience does. Negative attitudes towards the "other" have important root causes, but, at least in the case of the Holy Land, there is one factor that makes it possible for these causes to induce the negative attitudes, and without this factor they would just disappear. This is very similar to the fact that, despite the root cause of the force of gravitation, the computer I use for the writing of this article does not fall down to the floor when there is a table beneath it. In our activities of the IEA we find again and again that, in the case of the human relations in the Holy Land, the equivalent for the lack of a table is the lack of real knowledge of the other, simply ignorance. Profound understanding of the other opens the door for mutual respect, trust, and even friendship—despite the disagreements that continue to exist.

Imagine a group of Muslim and Christian Palestinians coming from Nablus, Ramallah, or Bethlehem, to meet a group of Israelis in an interfaith encounter. Most of these people, in both groups, have never met the other before, and nearly all their knowledge about the other comes from the media. During the height of the second intifada that meant that they "knew" for sure only one thing: that the other was trying to, or at least dreaming of, killing them. Still, when they agree to follow the guidelines of the interfaith encounter, they go through the process of discovering the humanity of the other through a deep and sincere discovery of the other's religion and culture. It is amazing to see how quickly they connect, how fast they actually overcome prejudices and fears and replace them with respect and friendship. At the end of the second day, after they have met each other, taken part in two thematic conversations, and witnessed the Muslim and Jewish prayers, they all sing and dance together, or tell jokes at a social evening. When the time comes to bid farewell on the third day, they hug each other with tears and wish the next encounter would come rapidly.

The relations that were built have survived, in many cases that we know of, even some very difficult challenges that, unfortunately, were not rare in the last few years. In the context of our conflict, I believe that it is very encouraging to realize that once we overcome the ignorance between the different groups, we build a barrier that does not allow the root causes to induce prejudices, fears, and hatred. Another optimistic thought is that, if the fears and hatred can be overcome so easily, the Israeli-Palestinian conflict is probably not as deeply rooted as we think.

Describing the Process

How does it actually work? What is the content of the process? What is its framework? The content is composed mainly of interactive interfaith dialogue. It is important to stress that in the case of IEA, interfaith dialogue is not our goal but our vehicle to achieve the goal of true coexistence. We find that our work to overcome the conflict is most effective when we do not discuss the conflict. Instead, when we come together we encounter each other—whether religious or not—through the aspect of our respective religious traditions. As an alternative to political discourse—which very often tends to be very superficial and divisive—we offer the interactive interreligious discourse, which gives a lot of space for relaxed exchange between participants and is very effective in supplying the deep and positive interaction that is needed to overcome the attitude of ignorance. It invites its participants, religious or not, to come to the conversation from a deeper place in themselves. It reveals many similarities between the different traditions, which creates a basis for a sense of connection. But perhaps most important: it allows for a sincere joint conversation about the *differences*, and in this way its participants train themselves to accept the other as "an other"—someone who is different. In this way we promote our ability to develop friendships that are not conditioned by agreement.

In terms of framework we work with two main models. The first model can be described as a kind of positive shock treatment. Participants come together for two or three days of very concentrated encounter with the other, away from their homes. During these days of intensive encounter they engage in long and deep conversations about the perspectives of the different traditions on the theme selected for the retreat; they have the chance to witness the prayer of the other and sincerely share their views, feelings, and deliberations. They also have the opportunity just to have fun together or chat informally on the lawn or during meals. Through this encounter they overcome many of their misconceptions about the other and most of their negative attitudes. This model is a very powerful first exposure to the other and, in the current reality, in many cases is our only option.

The second model is the ongoing work of groups from different religious contexts in a given area or city that come together for regular interfaith encounters with each other. The work of the group starts as a joint center for interfaith encounter but develops a strong sense of one community in its participants. This mini-community both exemplifies to the larger communities how it is possible to coexist in harmony with respect for each other's unique identity, and as a growing seed of such relations that hopefully will grow to include the whole of the larger community.

Dialogue While the Occupation and Terrorism Continue?

Some may wonder: how is it possible for Palestinians to engage in relaxed dialogue while occupation continues and for Israelis to do the same when terrorism continues? We believe that this kind of work is the *only* way to overcome both in a sustainable way. In such a small land as the Holy Land, total separation between the two peoples is not a long-term option. Yes, it is possible to disengage here or build a wall there. It is even possible to use a window of opportunity to sign an agreement named after this or that European city. But none of these moves, and no political arrangement, can ensure a sustainable and enduring end to occupation and terrorism, and their replacement by peace, without the real building of good relations between the two peoples. And when the respectful and friendly relations are built, political arrangements will be able to endure and ensure true peace between the two peoples.

To conclude: what I am saying is that by gaining true, deep, and sincere knowledge about each other, we build in ourselves a "security fence" that, instead of separating us from one another, defends us against negative attitudes. What is left to peacefully develop in our hearts are mutual respect, friendship, and love. These, in turn, will create room for a growing harmony between the communities and will build a solid foundation for the sustainability of future political agreements between them.

ABOUT THE CONTRIBUTORS

FARID ABDEL-NOUR is professor of political science at San Diego State University, California.

DR. SAMI ADWAN is a lecturer in the Faculty of Education, Bethlehem University.

DR. MUSTAFA ABU SWAY is associate professor of Philosophy and Islamic Studies at al-Quds University.

DAN BAR-ON and SALIBA SARSAR grew up on opposite sides of the Israeli-Palestinian divide. Bar-On is professor of psychology at Israel's Ben Gurion University of the Negev and co-director of PRIME (Peace Research Institute in the Middle East), in Beit Jala, PNA. Sarsar is associate vice president for academic program initiatives and associate professor of political science at Monmouth University, New Jersey, US.

DANIEL BAR-TAL is professor of social psychology at the School of Education, Tel Aviv University. He served as the president of the International Society of Political Psychology. His work focuses on the psychological foundations of intractable conflicts. The present article is a summary of one chapter in a book he co-authors with Professor Yona Teichman about Arabs' stereotype and prejudice in Israeli society.

HANNA BIRAN, a clinical psychologist and organizational consultant, lectures in the Department of Psychotherapy in the Medical School at Tel Aviv University, and is a member of IMUT (Mental Health Professionals for Promotion of Peace).

Dr. John Bunzl is the Middle East expert of the Austrian Institute for International Affairs and a lecturer in Political Science at the University of Vienna. He is co-editor, with Prof. Benjamin Beit-Hallahmi, of *Psychoanalysis, Identity and Ideology: Critical Studies on the Israel/Palestine Case* and editor of *Islam, Judaism and the Political Role of Religions in the Middle East.*

Eugenio Chahuán is professor of history and director of the Center of Arabic Studies at the Faculty of Philosophy and Humanities, the University of Chile.

Abdelmajid Charfi is a renowned Islamic thinker and author. He teaches at Manobah University, Tunis.

Akiva Eldar is the *Ha'aretz daily* diplomatic affairs analyst.

Alexander Flores is Professor of economy, society and language of the Arab World, the University of Bremen, Germany.

Sander L. Gilman is professor of liberal arts and sciences at Emory University.

Sivan Hirsch-Hoefler and Eran Halperin work at Haifa University's National Security Studies Center.

Dr. Meir Litvak is a senior lecturer at Tel Aviv University's Department of Middle Eastern and African History.

Dr. Nadia Nasser-Najjab is an expert on issues of conflict resolution and peace education. She is a member of the Palestine-Israel Journal editorial board.

Dr. Laila Nazzal, a former professor at the University of California, Los Angeles, and a fellow at the Aspen Institute for Humanistic Studies, is currently teaching at the Brigham Young University, Jerusalem Center for Near Eastern Studies.

PROF. NAFEZ NAZZAL currently teaches at the Brigham Young University, Jerusalem Center for Near East Studies. He is the author of *The Palestinian Exodus from the Galilee, 1948*, and has had articles published in many books and periodicals.

PROF. DINA PORAT is Head of the Stephen Roth Institute for the Study of Contemporary Racism and Anti-Semitism, Tel-Aviv University.

IMAM DR. ABDULJALIL SAJID is chairman of the Muslim Council for Religious and Racial Harmony, UK.

DR. YEHUDA STOLOV is executive director of the Jerusalem-based Interfaith Encounter Association (IEA).

ZIAD ABU ZAYYAD is Co-Editor of the *Palestine-Israel Journal*. A lawyer and journalist, he was a minister in the Palestinian Authority and a member of the Palestinian Legislative Council.

HILLEL SCHENKER is Co-Editor of the *Palestine-Israel Journal*. A journalist and editor, he is a veteran commentator on Israeli and Israeli-Arab affairs for the Israeli and international media.

PALESTINE-ISRAEL JOURNAL
STATEMENT OF PURPOSE

The *Palestine-Israel Journal* is an independent quarterly that aims to shed light on, and analyze freely and critically, complex issues dividing Israelis and Palestinians. It also devotes space to regional and international affairs. The Journal's purpose is to promote rapprochement and better understanding between peoples, and it strives to discuss all issues without prejudice and without taboos.

Based in Jerusalem, it is a unique, joint venture edited and produced by a group of prominent Israeli and Palestinian journalists and academics, on a totally egalitarian basis. You can find out more about the Journal at our website: www.pij.org.

—The Editors

"*The* Palestine-Israel Journal *provides a valuable opportunity for sustaining a process of communication essential to genuine peacemaking.*"
DR. HANAN ASHRAWI, *Palestinian spokeswoman*

"*The* Palestine-Israel Journal *undoubtedly fills an important gap in the literature. You can count me among your admirers.*"
SAMUEL W. LEWIS, *former U.S. ambassador to Israel*

"*For many years now, the* Palestine-Israel Journal *has proven itself an extremely useful, reliable source, providing analyses and important insights that enrich our understanding of the complex Israeli-Palestinian conflict and, hopefully, can guide the parties toward a peaceful resolution.*"
PROFESSOR GALIA GOLAN, *Emerita, Hebrew University of Jerusalem*

"*The* Palestine-Israel Journal *accords with the essential thrust of peacemaking in the Middle East. Peace will not be decided by politicians, but will evolve through grassroots engagement in such confidence-building measures.*"
PROFESSOR BERNARD LOWN, M.D., *Nobel Peace Prize, 1985*